UNDERWING

Also by Jennifer Lane

The Wheel: A Witch's Path to Healing Through Nature
The Witch's Survival Guide: Spells for Healing From Stress and Burnout

Titles for younger readers
The Black Air
The Second-Hand Boy

UNDERWING
A Story of Motherhood, Loss and Wild Intuition
JENNIFER LANE

First published in the United Kingdom by September in 2026

September, an imprint of Duckworth Books Ltd
1 Golden Court, Richmond, TW9 1EU, United Kingdom
www.septemberpublishing.org

Copyright © Jennifer Lane, 2026

All rights reserved. No part of this publication may be reproduced, stored in a retrieval system, or transmitted, in any form or by any means electronic, mechanical, photocopying, recording or otherwise, without the prior permission of the publisher.

The right of Jennifer Lane to be identified as the Author of this Work has been asserted by her in accordance with the Copyright, Designs and Patents Act 1988.

Page ix, extract from *If Women Rose Rooted: A Life-Changing Journey to Authenticity and Belonging* by Sharon Blackie, September Publishing 2016.

A catalogue record for this book is available from the British Library

Typeset by PDQ

Printed and bound in Great Britain by CPI Ltd, Croydon, CR0 4YY

The authorised representative in the EEA is Easy Access System Europe, Mustamäe tee 50, 10621 Tallinn, Estonia.

1

Trade paperback ISBN: 9781914613500
eISBN: 9781914613517

For Will, Linnet and Sky

Contents

Chapter 1	1
Chapter 2	6
Chapter 3 – Rook	19
Chapter 4 – Curlew	37
Chapter 5 – Familiar	56
Chapter 6 – Fox	78
Chapter 7 – Augury	102
Chapter 8 – Hare	124
Chapter 9 – Ladybird	142
Chapter 10 – Deer	161
Chapter 11 – Cat	183
Chapter 12 – Crow	201
Acknowledgements	217
Useful Organisations	221
Further Reading	223
References	225

You'll realise then, if you have not learned it before, that darkness is not simply a lack of light. Darkness is alive, and its life is obscured by light. Darkness puts out its tentacles and touches your face; darkness licks at your eyes and grants you a different kind of sight. Darkness is the voice of the shadow, a voice which words can only fail. Listen. Is it the drumming of your own heart that you hear, or the long, slow heartbeat of the Earth? Reach out, and there is nothing there. There is only you, whatever you might be, face-to-face with the long dark.

from *If Women Rose Rooted* by Dr Sharon Blackie

Chapter One

November 2023

I was five months pregnant when the scans started to show that something was wrong.

At the routine twenty-week anatomy scan on 16th November, I untucked my top and vest from my skirt and eagerly awaited the freezing jelly to be dolloped onto my stomach.

It is the last physical sensation I remember from that day.

The rest is a blur.

'The baby's bowel is dilated,' the ultrasound technician kept repeating while I stared wide-eyed and silent, hoping for an explanation yet receiving nothing. 'The baby's bowel is dilated.' We were shuffled into the midwife's office and told the same thing again and again on a looped and sinister backing track. No words of comfort. Just a white density on the monitor that no one would explain to me. I couldn't reply, just sat staring at them like a wind-up doll with a hand clasped to the smooth swell of my abdomen. The curve was so calm on the outside; just an expanse of pale stretched skin betraying nothing of the avalanche of problems that would soon be revealed inside. We left through the ward's contractor exit so as not to scare the other mothers in the waiting room.

Five and a half months is a long time to get to know someone. I've known people who have met and married in less. Five and a half months is half a year at university. It's a job contract. It's a whole prison sentence. It's enough time to change your life forever.

'I can't believe this is real,' I said a week later in the pale purple hospital room they used to confirm bad news. The door was cracked as they told us, my cries obvious, loud and feral to every couple sat frozen outside.

Our baby was incredibly sick.

The sickest a baby can be.

On hearing the news and suspected diagnosis, the edges of my vision dimmed and frayed; my world narrowed. The structure that had stitched my life view together was dismantled. This wasn't what happened to normal people. This shouldn't be happening to me. As I clutched my belly, I felt like we were two hearts beating in the darkness – mine, whole; hers, irreparable. My world became small enough to fit in the grasp of her ghost-white hand against the black monitor screen.

Then came the long limbo days while we waited for confirmation of the diagnosis. My husband, Will, went to work; his form of coping. I stayed at home. I stared at the walls and forgot to eat. Endless hours. Invasive tests. Stark-eyed nights that lasted an age. I rubbed my round, taut belly where the doctor had withdrawn amniotic fluid through a long, thin needle and thumbed the painful bruise the procedure had left.

All my life, I'd prided myself on being a morning person – solar-powered – jumping out of bed and thrusting my legs into yoga pants to catch the sunrise from the top of the hill, or to take my binoculars out to the lake and watch a raft of lapwings quick-step across the shore. These were the things I did to keep myself sane in the face of life's minor inconveniences. Nature was always there to heal me, to reset me after a missed deadline, a run-in with internet trolls or a panic attack brought on by the caffeine I needed to power through my endless, heavy workload. The earlier I left the house, the more potent and untapped nature's powers would be and I could allow them to settle on my face like silvery motes of tree pollen sent over a bridge from some other world. I had woven the dawn into my bones in my many years as a hiker, birdwatcher and practising Pagan to the point where my happiness depended on those first rays.

But after that moment, everything changed. The fragile balance of the world had tipped out of my favour.

I began to spend all my time indoors, like I had forgotten how the light transformed my skin; how the soft, fair hairs on my arms would turn golden in the late-autumn sun if only I could brave the cold and roll up my sleeves. It was like I'd been trapped in my bed by a blizzard. I blotted out every dappled smudge of light and kept the curtains sealed shut like an envelope gummed shut. A letter containing catastrophic news.

I turned the baby books upside down and tucked the twelve-week ultrasound behind my wedding photo on the mantelpiece. Time moved in slow, painful seconds that felt like kitchen knives dragging across the outer membrane of my brain. They say there are no words to describe the horror of such news, but I knew the words and they were all expletives I wanted to scream at full volume across the room.

While waiting for the inevitable diagnosis, there was just one thing that made me smile. Wherever I sat, feet tucked under an anvil weight of blankets, my cat Linnet would be lying next to me. Whenever I had to switch on my laptop to fend off the emails that kept on coming regardless, she would scuttle across the floor at full pelt, crashing into cardboard boxes in an attempt to make me laugh, and chasing jingly pockets of fabric across the laminate floor. Linnet usually hated being picked up and would purposefully get her claws stuck in our jumpers just so she could hiss and break our skin, but she suddenly morphed into a calico angel. Her purr became three times louder than usual. Researchers have found that cats purr at a frequency between 25 and 150 Hz, the same range shown to speed up bone knitting, pain relief and wound healing – the vibration of renewal.[1] It seemed Linnet could sense I needed more than just the usual head boops to keep me afloat while she worked overtime as my personal nurse.

How could I not smile at that?

That is the magic of animals. Their knowingness. Their ability to sense the subtle shifts in the world. In humans, we call it intuition, a thing of superstition and psychic ability. We pay good money for people to read us and tell us the colour of our aura. Animals – so much more rooted to the natural world than we could ever hope to be in the twenty-first century – are our link to the wild and a past version of humanity that once knew how energy truly works. They are perhaps even our link to the spirit world itself. I could feel Linnet's aventurine-coloured gaze penetrating my skull, softening my hospital-lined thoughts – with their bright flashing lights and sterile sonograph beeps – and trying to convey some hidden knowledge that I could not yet understand.

I slow-blink at Linnet as she sits, Sphinx-like and stoic in her favourite armchair, letting my eyelids mimic the soft catlike motion. *Thank you. I need you.* She blinks back. *I've got you, Mother. This is what I'm here for.*

In that time between hospital appointments, when nothing existed except Netflix specials, beans on toast and my own hot, shallow breathing, Linnet was always there watching me with those knowing green eyes from atop her yellow cushion.

My link to the natural wild world in a home that was quickly gathering dust.

Chapter Two

Thwack.

Cackle.

Pop pop.

The single magpie landed on my garden fence and bowed deeply to the kitchen window.

Some not-so-secret voice in my head said, 'This feels like a sign.'

I opened the window to frighten it off – a thing that I, the avid birdwatcher, had never done before in my life – and watched the magpie emit a series of machine-like *pops* as it soared away across the tree line. Something about those chess-piece feathers said, *Bad news ahead*, and I didn't like it. Had I ever seen a single magpie in the garden before? Maybe. I only remembered their chattering pairs performing acrobatics on the bird feeders, which always made me giggle and watch in wonder, or the sets of three that played around and pecked at the lawn as I pressed a hand to my belly.

Three for a little girl.

A deep crinkle appeared between my eyebrows. My head had been so distracted with my self-imposed hectic schedule for months now – saying 'yes' to every work opportunity even if it meant I had to stay in bed for two days recovering afterwards – that what if I'd missed them? What if there had been more of those single magpies out there? My nose had been stuck so doggedly to my computer screen that I had only seen the black and white of neat Calibri letters and not the flurry of feathers. Perhaps there had been a steady trickle of single magpies tracking sigils across my lawn since our positive pregnancy test, all of them going unseen as I worked into the night and forgot to go outside, oblivious to the lone chequered venturers across my patio.

What if the world had been showing me the signs? And, in my busyness, I had ignored them.

An omen, I thought.

The word 'omen' – an event that is thought to tell something about the future – hasn't always predicted something bad; yet, over time, the term has become synonymous with the ominous: the broken mirror, the unexpected comet and the doomed job interview scheduled for Friday the thirteenth. Humans have been watching out for omens since the dawn of civilisation in Ancient Mesopotamia, desperately hoping to change their dismal luck around. They believed that omens were signs of the will of the gods and it was our job to clock them and set ourselves on the path of right once more.

The practice of this sinister form of divination has been passed down the generations through Babylon, Ancient Greece and Ancient Rome to the present day, sometimes written down but mainly through the oral tradition. In the early twentieth century, a Mandaean priest in Ahwaz, Iran, spoke of the aeons-old astrological knowledge transmitted from priest to priest in secret throughout time. He said:

> If a raven croaks in a certain *burj* [an astrological house] I understand what it says, also the meaning when the fire

crackles or the door creaks. When the sky is cloudy and there are shapes in the sky resembling a mare or a sheep, I can read their significance and message. When the moon is darkened by an eclipse, I understand the portent: when a dust-cloud arises, black, red, or white, I read these signs, and all this according to the hours and the aspects.[2]

Over time, some began to believe omens were signs of fated events we could not change, while others used amulets and magical protections to keep themselves safe. Even up until recently, knowledge of omens was widely recognised and taken seriously but is now largely coated in the same cloth as superstition and old wives' tales (as if those wives hadn't been noticing and sharing their citizen-science wisdom for centuries). The practice of omen reading and divination is still a large part of a modern-day Pagan practice – a path I have been following since I was just twelve years old – with many Pagans heading straight to their Tarot decks to predict the future. What will the cards show today? The Star (hope)? Or the Tower (destruction)?

It is a system of knowing that the witch in me believes with all her heart.

But only the most common omens have persisted into everyday culture.

The old rhyme goes:

One for sorrow, two for joy,
Three for a girl, four for a boy,
Five for silver, six for gold,
Seven for a secret never to be told.

*

If you'd ever wondered, the rest of the rhyme goes:

> Eight for a wish, nine for a kiss,
> Ten for a bird you must not miss.
> Eleven for health, Twelve for wealth.
> Thirteen beware, It's the devil himself.
> Fourteen, make your choice, Fifteen, take your pick,
> Sixteen, the sweetest, Seventeen, your heart's wish.
> Eighteen for a letter, Nineteen for better,
> Twenty, the future, It's now or never.

This version has been written in the British history books since 1820, but is likely to have existed for centuries longer, meaning people have been shooing away the threat of sorrowful magpies for hundreds of years. The 'original', however – documented in 1777 – goes:

> One for sorrow,
> Two for mirth,
> Three for a funeral,
> Four for a birth.

Which brings a whole new meaning to those clusters of three.

A past, in-tune, version of me would have noticed the signs. She would have honed in on the magpies, as well as the owl calls so close to the house that they made us jump. The old me would have listened out for the black cat that sang to Linnet from the shadows of the fuchsia bushes every evening, crouched ready with a water pistol in hand. When had I clamped shut the dark, heavy-lidded eye inside me that had always been so adept at spotting the glimmers of magic within nature, seeing signs of Mother Earth everywhere I went? If I'd been more observant, was there something I could have done to prevent all this?

What else had I missed?

I flicked my mind back to all the signs the Universe might have been trying to give me over the past five months. The debilitating first-trimester symptoms; the feeling of dread that seeped over me from week five of my pregnancy, and the frenzied, unsettled working. Had this all been just hormones? Or an alarm call?

With a searing flash, I thought of the rooks. The rooks I saw in their droves in Ireland in the month we conceived. The crows. The jackdaws. All those carrion birds that we remarked upon because of their unusual numbers. All harbingers of death. All 'the thing with feathers'.

A warning.

Sky was stillborn on the morning of 6th December 2023, at twenty-three weeks and three days old.

She didn't look like what Google had told me to prepare for but I asked the midwife to tell me what to expect before she put Sky in my arms. Just in case.

'She's perfect,' she said with tears in her eyes. 'She's perfect.'

She just looked like a little baby. Just a little baby sleeping. The only way we could tell she had been sick or was any different to the other babies I heard crying relentlessly down the ward was her extra toes. Six on each curled foot.

'Oh, sweetheart,' I remember saying. Then turning to Will amidst the blood splatter of the room and adding with joy, 'She has your nose!' I thought she really suited his nose.

The next few hours swam by in a haze of morphine – I'd been able to have the maximum dose because my baby had already been dead inside me but it meant I was high as a kite during the most impactful moments of my life. The midwives looked at me out the corners of their eyes because I wasn't acting appropriately. I was joking one second ('Don't fall asleep,' I said to Will. 'What if they send us home with the wrong baby?'), catatonic the next. I must have been in shock, with the drugs fighting the maternal sepsis that ripped through my body adding to the feeling of a weightless fugue state. I held her, then placed her down, picked her up again, unsure what I should do, who I was or why I was here. Then I slept – long dreamless hours when I could have been holding my baby but was knocked out by a heavy curtain of sleep that only deprivation and septicaemia could induce. In the afternoon, hazy and still reeling from the hard drugs that filled my system, I finally agreed for her to be taken away. I sagged back into the narrow bed as the specially designed 'cold cot' that kept her body cooler than room temperature rounded the door frame and turned down the corridor. I realised then I had not said half the things I wanted to say. Things like, 'I'm so, so sorry' for the hundredth time, and 'I wish we could have had more time together.' Instead, I just lay there and stared at the purple butterflies painted onto the walls of the 'compassionate delivery suite' – the now Sky-less room – and tried to ignore the many-tasselled cannula sticking out of my right hand.

Since the dawn of time, humans have had a compulsion to use animal symbolism. We have attached meaning to the creatures around us, enmeshing their lives with ours in a way that often doesn't seem fair to the poor beasts. People have invited them into our folklore, myths and fireside tales, branding ourselves with their traits – as mighty as a stag, as swift as an eagle. We love to cloak ourselves in their boldest characteristics in an attempt to give ourselves a place in the world. These symbols are never far from the forefront of my mind. In her truly stunning book *Windswept: Life, Nature and Deep Time in the Scottish Highlands*, Annie Worsley talks about the intriguing sea eagle remains found buried amongst the human dead within her local prehistoric burial grounds:

> It was easy to understand their passion for the great birds. Sea eagles are immense and beautiful. They exude power and strength: the very traits that prehistoric peoples would have desired for themselves and their families. They may have expected protection from the birds in return for such reverence. Sensations of wildness and power ... might well have accompanied their own encounters and been important to the ancient communities, while gathering remains reinforced physical and spiritual bonds with the birds over many generations and perhaps reaffirmed societal connections to nature and the living world ... the consensus is that such connections with a particular animal or bird species not only existed, they were important.[3]

For me (and the 75,000 self-identifying Pagans in the UK), there is an understanding that every living thing has a supernatural medicine to give – be it the strength of the oak, the grace of the deer or the wiliness of the fox: some call it magic.

Butterflies – painted, etched and stitched into every corner of this hospital room – have long symbolised hope, transformation and the flight of the soul. Across so many cultures, butterflies with their stained-glass colours and gentle flutterings have woven themselves into our stories of hopefulness and peace, gathering up the souls of the dead to carry them peacefully to the next step of existence. The light of the Otherworld through the wings of a butterfly must be a wonderful sight for all those shell-shocked spirits. Psyche, the beautiful Greek deity with her butterfly wings, is the goddess of the soul. She was sent to Hades to overcome many challenges and won her reward – immortality. She would live forever in marital bliss in the arms of her husband, Eros, the god of love. A fate befitting a butterfly queen.

I thought about how different the tone of this hospital room would be if those butterflies had been moths. The butterfly's night-time cousin, moths have always drawn the short straw. Lepidopterophobia is the fear of butterflies and moths but we most often see it attributed to moths – the ghostly representatives of death. Those translucent wings with their smattering of night-time dust can evoke panic in even the most sensible of people, and folklore tells us that if a moth flies into a candle flame and snuffs it out, someone in the house will shortly die.

The contrast between a day- and night-time animal can sometimes make all the difference to our stories. A dream or a nightmare. A hope or an omen.

The thought sent a prickle up my spine.

With all my knowledge of the natural world, I'm so angry at myself that I hadn't read the omens, at my blustering ignorance.

I'd cut myself off so far from the natural world that I hadn't even realised it until the ultrasound tech looked at me with fear glazed in her eyes.

This wasn't me.

I had spent so many years learning to read and connect with the Earth, and to treat it with the respect it deserves. I even wrote my first book, *The Wheel*, all about returning to ancient magical customs, the slow turning of the Wheel of the Year, and interpreting the rich symbolism of the Earth by divining the secret messages it is trying to convey.

But right then in my hospital bed, I was lost. I didn't know how this disconnection had happened. The world's cycles have failed me here – this is not the order of things.

Children should never be the first to pass. The womb should not be a portal to the underworld.

When I arrived home a day later – having still been septic through the night – I lay in the spare room on the only bed that didn't hurt my newly widened hips and tried to regulate my temperature and my tears, but my mind was a disjointed sludge of memory. I caught snatches of lyrics that would be played at her funeral and the kindly tones of the midwives' platitudes. It had been days since I'd been outside in fresh air; my usual coping mechanisms of walking and birdwatching swept under the dark covering of stillness that had engulfed us.

Another memory flashed up. Sky's still, pink face resting in the cupped palm of my hand.

I guessed this is what PTSD must feel like.

*

Recently, before all this had happened, I had become interested in somatics – the study of the mind–body connection; how everything we experience shows up in the body in some form or another. In *When the Body Says No*, renowned doctor Gabor Maté said: 'Emotions that are suppressed do not disappear, they manifest in the body as illness', with difficult experiences showing as pain, inflammation and disease.[4] I had marvelled at the knowledge of how trauma is stored in the physical body rather than just the mind and how journalling or talking therapy coupled with somatic movement, like walking, yoga, dancing or tai chi, can help us to process our trauma in the most effective way, moving it through and out of the body like stormy waves bursting their flood barriers. All the hiking I had done over the years suddenly made sense. Whenever I had had periods of depression, anxiety or stress, walking was the only thing that had helped; the steady thrum and pulse of my steps harmonising the hemispheres of my brain, creating a humming that tuned out the dread and crushed my uncomfortable feelings under the heel of my hiking boot.

In bed, I rolled over and groaned, pain-free movement feeling a long way from me.

Some resigned part of me knew that to process this trauma – and trauma it most certainly was – I would have to get moving at some point. I'd have to maybe pick some distant hiking trail like any good nature writer would do, head into the wilderness to find out some big truth, emerging stronger in mind and spirit, wearing sponsored neon hiking gear.

But I didn't want to move. I didn't want to go places where she hadn't been.

And besides, I knew the truth now anyway: life is so incredibly moth-thin. It is so delicate and precious. So much can go wrong in those very first vital moments, so we must celebrate it as much as we can because it is an absolute miracle that any of us are here at all.

For me, I felt there was nothing else left to discover.

A tawny owl began a one-sided conversation outside the window. Maybe some faint reply came over an otherworldly divide – but I didn't hear it. My channel to the spirit realm had turned to static and then gone black but I knew well enough from my years of witchery that an unanswered owl's cry nearby meant illness and death were coming to someone in the house.

In all honesty, right then, I wished it would be me.

'Enough,' I said. 'Enough.'

I palmed a small round dose of zopiclone and shifted fitfully into sleep.

The next day, my eyes felt raw as torn flesh. As if they had tried to sew themselves up in my sleep so I wouldn't have to see any reminders of what has just happened. By waking, I had destroyed all their hard work.

With a sigh of relief, I realised it was well into mid-morning and I was still cuddling the sky-blue rabbit I had fallen asleep with.

A robin peeped on the bird table through the curtains, wondering why its usual supply of mealworms had disappeared in recent weeks. It wanted the reliability it had become used to. The natural order of things.

The reality was that what had happened to us was not outside of the world's natural order; it was just an awful slice of the cycle. However, we are not taught about how common this experience truly is. Losing a child is not a part of the modern human narrative we have constructed – one of meritocracy, where all good things come to those who wait, and where if we eat our greens, pay our bills and get our steps in, we can have all we've ever wanted. Or in this case, if we track our ovulation and take our pregnancy vitamins, we will be blessed with a healthy baby. The truth? I was not some civilised being far removed from nature because I drove a battered Mazda T3 named Timothée and obsessively curated Spotify playlists. I was not exempt from this big, terrible thing because I'd done everything that was expected of me.

I was a wild animal in the way a mother rabbit cannot always protect her kittens from the jaws of a fox, or how a blackbird cannot stop a blue-speckled egg from being flicked from the nest, only to be devoured by the crow hunkered below. My new and unfurling grief was an insight into the darkest corners of the forest and the horrors that happen there daily.

I too was part of all nature's cycles – the good bits and the paralysingly bad.

Easing myself up onto my elbow, I turned towards where Linnet was asleep at the end of the bed. She was a round, dark calico smudge in the folds of the duvet, soft and gently sighing through her pink, inquisitive nose. Was she taking on the role of shaman through her dreams, speaking to the ghost of someone small who barely ever existed? Maybe if I could fold myself back into nature, weave myself a seal-skin selkie coat or fashion a many-antlered mask, I too could slip through the worlds with her and say all those things I had meant to say in that hospital bed. I could let my daughter know what I didn't have the words for in my state of shock and sepsis.

Maybe tomorrow. Or the next day.

If this was going to be a journey, I wanted to write about rediscovering nature's signs, yes; but I also wanted to write about her – my Sky – even though I wasn't yet sure how to do that. Now that nature had cracked me wide open to the elements, I felt like I had to reforge my connection with it. My entire relationship with the world had just changed. Reconnecting with nature on an earth that had taken absolutely everything from me wasn't going to be easy but I knew I had to if I was ever going to live some semblance of a 'normal' life again. If my reading was anything to go by, I knew that nature – and walking through it – would be integral to my healing, helping me process the grief and trauma of my experience. Maybe I'd even find joy in it once more. But, more than anything, I wanted to write everything I knew about Sky, about the loss of something so precious, and how we as a society are so little prepared for the drastic reordering of life's most significant events.

For now though, I would stay here a while longer, clutching this cuddly rabbit to my chest in the almost-winter darkness, wondering how to start telling our story – mine and hers.

Chapter Three

Rook

The WhatsApp conversations continued. Flowed on. People's lives propelled forward. They sent me pictures of redwings and landscapes; articles about green tech; poodles pressing buttons that allowed them to speak; and how to make a peanut sauce. But what would they like from me in return? A spray of emojis perhaps.

'Wow! That's incredible. So beautiful.'

But answering seemed so utterly pointless. I had already seen the most beautiful thing in the world, and she had been wrapped in blue polyester in my arms. What more could I ever need to see?

Sky wasn't what we were going to name her originally. When she was still growing inside me, I had a list of names in my chaotic notes app amongst the recipes and book recommendations, the passwords to websites I would only ever use once and the jotted down dates of midwife appointments. I would go through this list religiously a few times a week, trying each one out in my mouth, testing for any trips or stumbles, any nicknames that school bullies might take advantage of. I'd write each one out in full, looking for how many loops of my cursive writing fell above or below the line. I had always liked names that fell with at least one loop below the line. But when we found out about Sky's condition and what we were now faced with, all of those names felt suddenly ridiculous. They were uncanny doppelgangers with half-smiling faces; little lives that didn't match hers.

Sky's name fell into my head as we lay quietly on the sofa just after her diagnosis, my fists curled on Will's chest. Three small letters, with one loop below the line. Such a small name for such a small girl. Will immediately agreed to the name and we quickly realised how often 'sky' comes up in conversation. Comments about the weather, the moon and getting out of the house before the sun went down all took on one hundred times their meaning. The sky felt bigger than we'd ever seen it before.

In her book *Grief Works*, about her experience of working as a grief therapist, Julia Samuel says:

> There is almost nothing more traumatic than the death of a child. It tears up the rule book of life ... of all the losses people suffer, it takes the longest to rebuild their lives afterwards ... They are forced to reconfigure their present lives as well as their idea of the future without their child in it.[5]

The curling slip of madness forming around the edges of my mind tells me that this is true. There is nothing that could possibly compare to this. Will doesn't seem to understand, no cells of insanity clustering together in his brain. As a father and not a mother, his experience was different than mine. He hadn't wanted to hold her and feel the lightness of her against him, which I didn't understand. How could he not want to hold this child we had created together – the one thing we had wanted for so long and pinned all our hopes on – and feel the snow-like softness of her baby skin? Maybe to him she was so small that her fragile body could be compartmentalised, put in a box and filed away under 'traumatic life events I'll deal with later'. But, as a mother, I had carried her inside me for all those months. I would always know the feel of her and I would always want to hold her close.

In all my flashbacks, I cradle her to me in the crook of my left arm. Her head is as heavy against me as it will ever be. Her glistening little hands are slightly curled, the weight of her feeling right and horribly wrong.

Such a beautiful baby girl. All mine. All gone.

I stopped engaging with the messages people sent. I sank into my grief for long, seamless weeks; tired of the blue website links and dodging the 'you'll come out of this stronger' comments.

I never wanted to be stronger. I just wanted to be a mother.

Early in life, I'd assumed everyone's families took them on romps across the cliffs amongst pink swathes of thrift when they went away and taught them the names of all the birds on Saturday mornings.

It is difficult to remember when my interest in birdwatching first started. Birds had been pretty much ever-present in my life, my dad having been a member of the YOC (the Royal Society for the Protection of Bird's first Young Ornithologist's Club) in the late 1960s and '70s. We'd stop off at bird hides whenever we could on holiday rambles and I had been able to name all the garden birds by the time I was nine thanks to the bustling feeders in my grandparents' garden.

Something I remember distinctly about my pastel-coloured childhood bedroom was the hard plastic poster above my desk that told me how to ID corvids. This didn't feel out of place in the slightest and I diligently learned about rooks, carrion crows and jackdaws while lying in bed like I was collecting the names of Pokémon. These classic omens of death watched over me as I slept amongst the posters of Leonardo DiCaprio and *Coronation Street* characters. It only dawned on me in my teenage years that this perhaps wasn't typical of the families on my terraced street. But it set me up nicely for craving the countryside and 'going on' about birds with my dad while visitors looked on in despair. I'm now thirty-four and my binoculars are hanging on a hook by my front door, just where I need them.

On my childhood poster, the rook lay in the bottom right-hand corner. It was the last bird on the chart, a sinister-looking thing with a pale bill that bled into its skull, the feathers at its base peeled back to reveal bare, grey cheeks and chin. The poster made it look like a ghastly creature that I would often look out for in my garden or in the park with some form of morbid glee. But seeing them in real life never really prepares you for the shock of it.

If ever there was a bird that looked like it came straight from the underworld, it's the rook. But it's the other corvids that get the worst rap.

In Irish mythology, the Morrigan is the goddess most associated with carrion birds. She is a shapeshifting figure clad in black and depicted either as a triad of goddesses or as a single entity with three distinct forms: Anu, Badb and Macha. Morrigan can be translated to Phantom Queen or Great Queen, an apt name considering her association with the lofty ideas of war, death and fate. In fact, she is so terrifying that I have never worked with her in my years practising witchcraft. Hecate – goddess of the night and underworld: yes. Cerridwen – goddess of death, rebirth and cauldron of fate: yes. But never the Morrigan.

On the Irish battlefields, her presence, when spotted, was enough to terrify warriors into paralysis, or it could inspire them to fight for their life. The fearsome queen of war would often appear to predict the outcome of conflicts: her raven companion came in very handy for this task. Ravens are the Cassandras of the bird world, offering prophecies and foretelling fates with a flick of their dark wings. Known for their ominous 'gronk' sound and surprisingly large stature – much, much bigger than their crow neighbours – the raven would collude with the Morrigan to foretell the fate of warriors on the battlefield.

Of course, Ireland is not the only country to have legends about corvids.

In many Native American cultures, the crow is revered as a symbol of intelligence, resourcefulness and transformation. Any of us who have watched them for even a short amount of time will have seen their cleverness and their skills with tools, patterns and human speech. Some crows have learned up to one hundred words and around fifty complete sentences, putting them on a par with preschool-age children. Linnet could never. In Hinduism, however, this glossy bird is associated with the goddess Dhumavati – one of the Mahavidyas, a group of ten goddesses considered manifestations of the divine feminine.

Dhumavati is the widow goddess – 'the smoky one' or 'the one who is composed of smoke' – depicted as an old, dishevelled woman riding on the back of a jet-black crow or a chariot that moves on its own, symbolising the relentless march of time. There are those that say her crow emblem is symbolic of her dark magic and the shadow forces of the world.

Clever, yes; tricksters, yes, but this is not the side of the crow, the rook or the raven that springs to mind when they loiter on the bare branches of the graveyard or carve shapes in the grey sky above the moors with their jagged wing tips. We can look at countless cultures and find corvids at the centre of myths and stories of destruction and death.

And their shadows seemed to follow our every move around Ireland.

Which is where this whole thing started.

Drogheda, Ireland, July 2023
'Two and a half hours?' Will said. 'I don't think it'll take that long. Ireland's quite a small place.'

Several hours into the hike, I was realising how wrong a person can be.

Many things had surprised me about this two-week trip.

From a long weekend in Dublin with Will a few years ago, I had assumed, very incorrectly, that Eire was an extension of the UK: the Tesco Metros on every street corner and pricey pints were a testament to this – in my mind, anyway. However, this was absolutely not the case outside of the city and – on our second visit to Ireland – I became quickly enraptured by, well, most things. The slower pace of life, the almost aggressive friendliness of everyone we met and, to top things off, the excellent public transport.

Definitely not like the UK at all.

For my thirty-third birthday, Will had booked flights and given me a trail of clues to solve that would lead me to the answer of where he was taking me, telling me he was going to reveal a new clue every week until I got it. Bubbling over with giddiness in the restaurant, I set about with a giggly tirade of ridiculous guesses. My tall, blond, frightfully stoic lawyer husband gave in and told me the answer in about twenty minutes.

The present was a two-week summer holiday to Ireland where we would be travelling around the country's Megalithic sites from Dublin to Drogheda, Sligo to Galway, then Limerick to Cork. Prehistoric monuments, hiking the coast, and finding the best birdwatching spots. Oh, he's a good 'un, my husband. Little witchy me had been mainlining Celtic mythology since I was twelve years old so, needless to say, I was pretty excited. Not only were we going somewhere I wouldn't overheat, as I usually – very embarrassingly – did anywhere abroad, but he had booked the ultimate Pagan holiday.

However, armed with only a bag of cheese sandwiches and some dodgy 4G, Will and I were on the 'two-and-a-half-hour' hike that probably needed six months of training. After a wrong turn that added a further two hours to our trip and then a hair-raising jog down an eighty-kmph winding road (no Right to Roam here), I genuinely didn't know if we were ever going to make it to our destination in one piece.

Newgrange. Ireland's oldest prehistoric monument.

My knees wobbled dangerously from fatigue and a shred of anxiety jagged at my chest. But this was a feeling I was quite accustomed to by now. From 2022 to 2023, there were times when I felt like I had been fighting for my life.

The reality was: I had written and published four books in three years – something I never dreamed I would be able to do – but it came with a sting in the tail. The rumours were true – authors needed at least a part-time job, but maybe two or three, in order to survive. And so, on top of my book-writing, promotion and nationwide events, this introverted author became a copywriter, a magazine sub-editor and a Reiki practitioner all at the same time just to pay the bills.

It turned out my lifelong dream was coming with a cost.

'You're always so busy!' people marvelled, admiring smiles showing me their molars. 'I don't know how you do it!'

Neither did I, to be honest.

As a result of the tight fist of control I kept over my workload, I lost seven pounds from my already gangling form, giving me a winceworthy BMI. My intense schedule guided my caffeine binges and long evenings at the screen. I started to lose my hair again, like I had in my late twenties when I was stressed out to the max. My skin was dull, I didn't see my friends and there were times when the constant whirring of my mind threatened to overtake me and sweep me under. There wasn't a moment of quiet to relax, to steep my anxiety in a hot bath, or to stick my head out the window and check for birds on the feeder. I had fast become very out of touch with the natural world and the Pagan beliefs that had sustained me for so long, chained to my desk often for twelve hours a day, seven days a week. The caw of an ominous crow could not have broken my concentration.

Yet, in every Instagram picture, I was smiling, even if my jaw did look like it could cut glass and my clothes flowed and bubbled around me to fill the empty space where nutrition and a bowl of chips should have been.

How utterly embarrassing to be a witch and an author writing about wellbeing and burnout, yet here I was, hovering dangerously on the verge of a breakdown with no end date in sight. I was really sick and I couldn't possibly let anyone know.

No wonder we hadn't conceived yet after seventeen months of trying.

'It can't be long now,' said Will with the false assurance of a man who had actually just cartwheeled over a fence to avoid being hit by a car. 'The map says—'

A rook hacked a caw from behind the hedgerow beside us and made us both jump.

'That better not be a sign,' I said, making my eyes bulge meaningfully.

However, Will and I rounded a corner and we finally saw what we had been travelling towards.

Newgrange glinted green and sparkling white over the hill and my chest fizzed under the July Irish drizzle. I took a crystal-cut gulp of air. This was the place I'd been dying to see and – even from a distance – I knew it was going to heal my stressed-out soul.

Located in County Meath in the northeast of Eire, Newgrange is one of the most well-preserved ancient Pagan sites in the country (but also possibly the world). Built during the Neolithic period in around 3200 BCE – making it older than Stonehenge and the Pyramids of Giza – this spectacular, round passage tomb and ritual site is coated in white quartz, making it a shining memorial to house the remains of the dead.

From my witchcraft practice and knowledge of shamanism, I knew that quartz is a great conductor amongst gemstones, harnessing the energy that is funnelled into it and amplifying it one hundred times. Perhaps the original guardians of Newgrange used quartz to add a protective layer to the site or maybe they used it to amplify the powers of their priests or the spirits that were housed inside. Whether that was with good or bad intentions, I didn't know – but I was excited to get a sense of the place. So ready was I to soak up that healing, strengthening quartz energy, and ask it to, maybe, pretty please, let my hair stop falling out.

If anywhere could restore me, it was going to be Newgrange.

The site was filled with light – I could see that even from our viewpoint two miles away. That quartz exterior really marked the place as a beacon of magic. Could there be anything more mystical than crouching inside the stone entrance and being hit with the first rays of winter-solstice dawn? The site's entrance perfectly aligns with the sun's trajectory once a year so that a narrow beam of light enters the passage and illuminates the inner chamber, leading scholars and historians to believe that Newgrange had ritual significance around the cycles of life and death – a brief and dazzling flash of light burning bright for a few moments before it is overtaken by yawning darkness once again: surely that is the ultimate symbolism.

The Irish really do death well.

Cairns, dolmens, passage tombs – the landscape is full of them, like a giant's leftover game of coffin marbles. Yet the markers are far from random, often covering the graves of chiefs and prominent figures in local clans. Newgrange itself was discovered to house the remains of noble families. One archaeologist working at Newgrange described what they found there as cathedrals built for a cult of the dead.

Indeed, Ireland's death reverence is surprising but what surprised me most was the rooks.

Rooks – I hadn't seen more than a handful of them in my life back home. In England, the ubiquitous carrion crows, jackdaws and magpies cackle with a tinge of mania up and down suburban streets, knocking blue tits off the bird table with a resolute 'wock wock'. I once saw a magpie perform a perfect pirouette on a swinging bird feeder like it had magically completed its transformation into a garden bird. While at university, I would often hop on a train and head out to the West Yorkshire moors between Hebden Bridge and Haworth – Ted Hughes country – and watch the crows with their black-fringed feathers and pops of ominous breath flying ragged across the barren landscape. They would change direction at will, folding in on themselves like jet-black origami paper and materialising on a new route as if an errant wind had taken them there. Perhaps this breeze was the breath of some old god, and they were merely responding to his messages.

But there in Ireland – everywhere – rooks had taken their place.

They clustered on the street corners of Cork, loitered on telephone wires and swooped low over the fields. Their bald, pale beaks protruded from their skulls like that of a plague-doctor mask – or as if the flesh on their cheeks was slowly deteriorating, gradually revealing a death mask of pure bleached bone. Whenever I spotted one, I felt like I was being watched by a shadow I just couldn't shake, one that pulled me in and repulsed me all at the same time, telling me to bend my head close and listen carefully.

I had seen plenty of carrion birds in my life but there was something about the rooks of Ireland that made my malnourished hackles rise. It was a feeling that made me wish I'd brought a charm against omens and bad things to come.

We finally arrived at the visitor's centre – a beautiful modern glass building with ornate metal bridges and statues curled into the shapes of silvery salmon with Celtic knots and twists.

'Two adults, please,' said Will, throwing on a charming smile to cover up how terrifyingly sweaty we both were.

The woman at the information desk raised her eyebrows. 'Have you booked?'

'Oh… no, we haven't. Is that going to be an issue?'

'Well, we're all booked up today.'

'Oh,' Will said.

'Oh,' I repeated, while a cartoon paperweight dropped from my chest into my feet. 'Is there any way we could just walk around the site?'

'No, the site is only accessible via one of our buses and we're booked up now until August.'

'August!'

We hovered.

Will asked what our options were but the conversation quieted in my head as I realised that I'd stopped breathing. I was holding all my remaining life force inside my lungs like I was waiting for it to multiply and erupt from my chest in a staggering scream. This – I noted in the back of my silent brain – was dangerous territory for someone who had been existing on the periphery of her sanity for the past year.

In a voice that would not have seemed out of place on a weary Disney princess, I said: 'I'm going to stand over here,' and wafted myself over to the floor-to-ceiling windows.

So, we didn't have a ticket. No big deal. Ireland has 187 known stone circles dating from 3300 to 900 BCE – plenty to go around. We'd just go to another one. There was probably one in the gift shop. But, no – this still felt like a kick in the gut. This had been my chance to reconnect and to stand in front of Ireland's largest Pagan monument to remind myself that I am still here – I still exist. We had walked so far to get here and I had promised myself I was going to place my hands on that cooling quartz exterior to let those old, old stones heal my bones, re-twist my DNA and make me whole again.

I was going to feel like myself for the first time in months.

Right?

We had been walking for so long that my knees were like inside-out umbrellas. I felt like an escapee who'd been running for weeks only to be refused a glass of water before my eyes fogged over.

Before I was able to stop myself, I began to cry.

'Stop it,' I muttered, in shock at my sudden tears.

But I cried and I cried and I cried.

I was numb with exhaustion from the full-day hike. And I was furious. With Will for not checking that we needed to book, and with myself for having this hugely ridiculous reaction.

He came and swept me up into a big squeeze, saying, 'I'm so sorry, I didn't realise how much you wanted to see this place.'

Neither did I, to be honest. But I did know just how much I had wanted that healing.

While I composed myself in the bathroom, Will asked how close we could get to the monument without a ticket and the staff members said not to bother. Will had other ideas and, with the confidence of a sniffer dog on the scent of a spring hare, said we were going to try anyway.

I knew there was a reason I loved him.

He led the way out of the visitor's centre but my legs didn't seem to work anymore. They were slow and trunk-like, plodding back along the metal bridge over the drifting River Boyne. Will was striding out ahead with renewed purpose, head and shoulders above everyone else around us, completely unaware of my pace, or lack of it. I was really trying but my body seemed to have given up. When I reached the other side, Will's blond head was out of sight and I ground to a halt.

I couldn't go any further. Defeated.

But then I heard it.

A high-pitched, melodious trill. Followed by what could be mistaken for a dog's squeaky toy coming from a copse of young trees to my right.

My head jerked up.

An infinitesimal movement caught my birdwatcher's eye in a birch tree.

There was a young goldcrest in there, revealed wholly to me through a circular gap in the tree's foliage. It sat, its right eye meeting mine – a silver-black pinprick amongst the shadows. It was singing at me as if I were a fellow cute dot of feathers and not a tear-streaked member of the human race.

So Ireland wasn't just full of death birds after all.

This is one of the northern hemisphere's smallest and daintiest birds. A tiny trilby of yellow feathers lies flat to its small, rounded head; I always think that the lines slanting out around their needle-thin beaks make goldcrests look like worried little ping-pong balls. If I wanted to, I could have reached out into the tree and plucked it out with my hand like Snow White. It was so close. So trusting. A messenger relaying its memorandum:

'You don't need old stones to feel connected. Just listen and you will find your home. *Trill, trill, trill.*'

In European folklore, goldcrests were said to bring good luck and blessings, bestowing happiness and prosperity on those who crossed their path. For the Ancient Celts, the goldcrest was a messenger from the spirit world, symbolising spiritual enlightenment and guiding people to the realms beyond or further along their spiritual path.

I felt my shoulder blades begin a series of clockwork motions, unrolling down my back. The sweetly pitched sound wound through the frayed threads of consciousness, weaving me back together again.

'Hey, you,' I said.

This moment was the first time I had felt connected to the natural world in almost a year and, if I hadn't just cried all my tears in a public bathroom, I would have let them out now. When had I last stood in a forest and put my hands on a tree to feel its energy answering mine? Or trampled across a moor and stretched out my senses to feel the soft, small creatures trembling below the heather line? When had I last left my house after sundown to call down the energy of the bare stars? All the things I had loved about being Pagan and feeling into the hidden pockets of the world had faded to a dim ember in my chest for way too long.

But that stops today, I resolved.

I stood listening to the bird's call for several minutes. I felt bound by some earthly decree to listen to every note this bird had to say.

I am listening, I wanted to call out. I hear you. I can be hopeful too.

In its song, I felt like I could see a flash of my old magical self.

'Jenn?'

Will had resurfaced from the conga of tourists, wondering where his sad, droopy wife has got to, and I waved to him with a renewed sense of pep. I was feeling shocked out of my numb state. The bird had come to remind me of what I had long suspected: moments of connection don't just appear when you enter a location of spiritual significance – they can come when we least expect it.

I thanked the goldcrest with a nod of my head – its song still working its magic on me.

'Are you OK?' Will puzzled.

Later that day (what's a few more thousand steps at this point?), Will and I arrived at Newgrange in all its sparkling glory and the kind woman behind the counter allowed us to sit in the picnic area and gaze at the monument. We arranged ourselves between the rooks that strutted there and she took a picture of us both together in front of the site – me in my sunglasses to hide my puffy eyes.

We sat for a long time until I began to feel the familiar prickles of otherworldly energy against my skin.

'Do you feel it?' I asked Will.

He frowned at the quartz monument. 'Yeah, there's definitely something about the place.'

This was a rare utterance from Will and I looked at him for a fraction longer in surprise. I'd come to expect an 'I'll tolerate your woo-woo silliness' response from my husband but this sentiment was new. Maybe in another ten years I'd make a trainee witch out of him after all.

I couldn't quite put my finger on the 'something' we could both feel but the swell of power surrounding the Newgrange site reached out to touch our sun-browned faces with velvet fingers and the feeling was like a balm for this up-and-down day.

The goldcrest's call, with its gently guiding light, came back to me – its healing had already begun before we reached Newgrange. Delicate, safe. Hopeful.

Then a sudden *clack* made me spin around.

A rook had landed on a stone wall behind me. It flattened its wings to its body and faced me. The slight hunch in its shoulders could have been a leer and the feathers at the base of its beak looked singed, burnt away to reveal even more of that grey, jutting bone.

There was no goldcrest melody on the breeze this time.

We stared at each other – this messenger of the Morrigan – black eyes meeting green. It seemed to be appraising me. Its darkness penetrated my pupils, keeping them pinpoint focused. I was stiff on the picnic bench as I awaited the rook's next move.

In spite of its appearance, this bird was gorgeous. So alien and striking; so commanding in its presence and in its hard *caw*. It didn't have the ethereal, shadow quality of a crow – it was stalwart and rooted in this world, as if layers of long-dead souls had compressed into a single being to make it as manifoldly solid and ageless as the stone around us. I wondered how many ancient souls the Morrigan had reaped on the nearby battlefields and how many of these the crows, rooks and ravens had transported to the Otherworld; how many this rook would transport in this lifetime. How many lifetimes had this one been holding its messenger role? I angled my chin up. It was a small act of defiance, one that said, 'Not today.'

The rook looked at me carefully, then Will, before glancing off to the left, its bill tilted upwards. I saw its hard white inner eyelid eclipse the black for one moment, like a full moon across a midnight lake, and then the rook was flying away in a rustle of feathers. Called back to the magical gates of its mistress.

For a moment I was frozen, spellbound and half clasped in the talons of the rook's spiny feet.

After a few moments, the babbling strains of a tour group faded slowly back into my consciousness. I stood, knees clicking, my jaw hard.

'Well, I didn't like that,' I said to Will as we got up to start the long, long journey back to Drogheda but I still felt the wisps of phantom fingers snagging my shoelaces, trying to snatch me back to the realm of the dead. I wondered what the bird was reporting back to the Morrigan on her dark throne. What intelligence did she glean from my defiant stare? What fate did she have in store for me?

Three days later, Sky's small, fragile cells would begin to form in my womb.

Chapter Four

Curlew

15 dpo BFN, no AF, white CM, CX high, BBT 36.52, TTC 2.5 years.

If you can't read this, perhaps you are one of the lucky ones.

The 'TTC (Trying to Conceive) Language' is filled with acronyms like these:

- DPO equals days post-ovulation
- AF stands for Aunt Flo (also known as a period)
- CM is cervical mucus (we talk about mucus *a lot*).

Then there's POAS (pee on a stick), FRER (First Response Early Result – a kind of pregnancy test) and the TWW (two-week wait after ovulation occurs). There are so many other abbreviations, all neatly recorded on message boards, in period trackers, in notes apps and in paper diaries like daily scientific equations. The chemistry of baby making. We write down our symptoms: every nosebleed, every abdominal twinge, every extra shot glass of saliva. We calculate due dates that never come to fruition. They come and pass, the veils of pastel-shaded 'welcome to the world' banners fading from our minds.

Those who have never experienced baby loss or infertility are unlikely to know this language. The code will be forever uncracked for them. And yet there is a whole internet underbody of message boards and desperate mothers-to-be, lost in this secret language, clutching their strings of TTC code and the receipts of their symptoms. Out in the offline world – because real life always keeps churning along – we wee on several sticks a cycle, squinting for that coveted second line. We throw the test away into the bathroom bin only to fish it out again two minutes later – just in case. We take our basal body temperature each morning. We attend other people's baby showers with a too-big smile. We can do a very good job of convincing ourselves that our PMS symptoms are early pregnancy signs. Every. Single. Month. We pass women in the street complaining that their child won't sleep through the night, we hear parents screaming at their child in the Tesco veg aisle, and in our minds we whisper quietly, 'You don't know how lucky you are.'

Some of us – if we really would dare to admit it – may whisper more loudly: 'You do not deserve to be a parent.'

We are clinging to the hope that one day a test might show us a BFP. A Big Fat Positive.

I should know.

I follow the message boards like I am the acolyte of some new cult, desperate to learn all I can that might make the founder bestow me with a special gift.

I had a glimpse of that gift once. But she was taken out of my grasp like I had fallen out of favour with the gods.

12 DPO.

13 DPO.

14 DPO.

Nevermind. Try again next month.

Lancashire, February 2024
It has been a long winter. An ugly, unwashed stretch of time.

In this limbo period, I do all the practical things:

I back up the photos of her on my phone. I call the funeral director and make arrangements. I put white flowers in vases. I fold away my maternity clothes and put them in a bottom drawer. I get a refund on my antenatal classes. I remember who I told about the pregnancy and send the appropriate messages. I chase up the midwives who never seem to remember our appointments. I ask Will to put the cot into the garage. I do half-hearted pelvic floor exercises. I put away the Christmas tree.

The constant stream of loving family, friends and baked goods has now faded to a trickle and my house, so recently filled with baby's breath and carnations from the conveyor belt of bouquets that arrived at our door, is empty and replaced with stagnant air. Closed windows, radiator dust and the quavering notes of stuck grief in my chest have turned the living room into something with a tight membrane I need to break free from.

I haven't emerged from the house much and my leggings feel loose around my waist, like I'm carrying a shed, empty skin from another life around my middle. Grief does amazing things to shift the baby weight (however, I wouldn't recommend it as a tried and tested diet).

Time and again, I go back to the fact that there is no word in the English language for a parent who has lost a child. There are words for the widowed and orphaned – those who have lost spouses and parents. But losing a child goes against the natural order of the world – perhaps we have not named it to keep the tempted hands of fate away from our door.

But who am I now on the other side of this threshold? What new secret name have I been gifted with?

I wonder how I should be feeling; how other childless mothers in the world might be faring at this point. Have they all taken a deep collective out-breath without me and resolved to get up and moving again? I still have the burnt-line reminder of my linea nigra coursing from my navel to my pubic ridge and, even now, my womb is contracting back down to its maiden size, causing me to wobble and double over in the hallway. Sleep is erratic, haunted by non-existent night feeds. My hips and lower back have fought through the constant rounds of sepsis antibiotics to regain their strength, so there is – physically – nothing keeping me inside anymore. Mentally? Well... I feel like a husk of dead skin. Realistically, how could anyone be faring any differently at this stage of the grieving game?

It has been nearly two months since the death of my daughter.

But today, I've finally come outside. Stop everything, everyone. She has emerged (and may scare small children).

I feel like a skittering fawn trying to find her centre of gravity for the very first time – and not necessarily succeeding. I forced my feet into my boots and left home about thirty minutes after dawn. Because I probably have to try to see a tree or something if I want to get this healing journey on the road, don't I?

Today is the first of February – the Pagan festival of Imbolc and a day I have celebrated for the past two decades of my life. In Celtic lore, this is a time of renewal and rebirth; of the first lambs and the first green shoots; Imbolc means 'ewe's milk' after all. This ancient fire festival is presided over by the goddess Brigid – the overseer of cattle, blacksmiths, poetry, women and childbirth; the maiden goddess with her angular childish face and a torch of Imbolc fire held aloft from her hand like a beacon of hope. Not to be rude to the great goddess but what does she know of childbirth?

In past years, I have performed elaborate Imbolc rituals to welcome the faint glimmers of spring and left cake and milk on my windowsill for the Fae. But today, I don't do either of these things. Today is a marker of the turning of time. We are already at the second Pagan festival since her death – how did that happen? As we click onto each spoke of the Pagan Wheel of the Year, I am reminded of how the celebrations keep dancing on and people plan meet-ups, pot-lucks and rituals to mark the passage of our important days; how the world transmutes and unfurls so quickly from the tightest Imbolc bud to the lush whorls of dog rose at Lammas. Time moves on.

The world doesn't wait long for the grieving, even though they themselves may feel frozen in time. So it is time to pick up my feet and pick up my life – or so I am told.

Here we go.

My hiking boots feel heavy, encrusted with five-year-old mud from the patchwork of the paths I have woven through my daily walks. If I cleaned my boots, they would lose their armour, their memories and their unique shape. After two months of abandonment, their solid feel is incredibly welcome.

The woods bordering the miles of open moorland near to my house are not a scary thing like in some German fairytale; they are man-made, young – not imagined up and twisted into shape by the earth's thorny fingers but carefully planned out, funded and licensed. The majority of the trees are birch, one of the easiest and fastest to grow – if you look at rewilded railway sidings you'll almost always find a jewellery box of silver birches embedded there as the average birch takes just two decades to reach a mighty eighteen metres in height. Glancing down at the roots of my local woodland, I can sometimes see the unfurled plastic casings trapped half-under the trees like shed spines. These remnants of their sapling days make me smile; a remembrance of the human hands that wanted to build this habitat out of nothing. The trees are mainly still spindles but I am so happy that thirty years ago someone thought to put this place here.

In November, when it gets dark so early in the woods, the night catches you unawares – you think you are just in the shade of the trees until you realise the light has been slowly peeling away everywhere else too. It leaves you blind; hands lurching to grab the next tree trunk to guide the way back to civilisation, like you have been chased into the ragged heart of the forest and will never find your way out. In midwinter, the wood's steep slopes are impassable, slick with mud and slushed-up leaf litter – so I can only imagine what it is like under these trees when the snow comes. Quiet, perhaps. Thick, folded silence. But in spring – oh-so-lovely spring – the woodland flowers thrive in the shady spots and I have been lucky enough to see a herd of deer passing reverently through here more than once. A few years ago, the RSPB had a slogan that said, 'If we build it, they will come.' That is exactly what has happened in this man-made wood.

I don't see any magpies, crows or rooks through the bare branches – only snatches of brown, fuzzed-over moor beyond – although I'm on high alert just in case. I wish I had a slingshot for any single magpies I might come across. But I wonder what other omens might be lurking around the birches.

Will and I moved out to the semi-rurality of East Lancashire during the pandemic. We've both said it was the best decision we ever made, although our friends might not know it. Every time we are asked where we live, we roll our eyes and say 'out in the sticks' then complain about the once-an-hour Northern Rail service and lack of takeaway options. But it's an act, a total lie. I love everything about where I live; the quiet dawns filled with swooping starling song, the sunset over the moor-swept hills and, most of all, the access to long, sprawling hiking trails that I've yet to find on any OS map. I am startled by just how many people – friends of friends, colleagues – would be terrified to move out of the city. Having lived in London, then Manchester for five years, with ready access to the gym, twenty-four-hour supermarkets and every kind of cuisine I could dream of – I know this is a whole way of life to give up. That life is full of easy, last-minute decisions; it is fast, urgent, exciting. Maybe even frantic. To some people, the idea of leaving this ready-when-you-are existence is horrific. Our town of choice is often met with confusion like I've just told people I teleport in from Easter Island every day. 'What made you move there?' they ask, as if I could only have made this life decision by force. I fight back the feelings of sadness when I hear this. Are people so disconnected from the countryside? Do they not miss the sound of birdsong? Are the quick-fix gains of city life so much more important than what has been lost by our move away from the country?

Here on the path, it is slow going. My breath is ragged and out of practice. I climb the slope and flip off the headphones

I've been wearing along the road to block out the sound. If only I had a nose plug to keep out the fumes too. My shoulders relax down a whole inch now that I have entered the arms of the trees and my cheeks feel lighter, ready to house a smile – maybe. I watch my feet as I skitter across the ridge where the first thoughts of bluebells are forming; it is slippery here and mud oozes out around my boots like I'm a pond-skater balancing on ripples. This is my favourite trail through the woods, as it is so rare to see another soul here.

Right now, the spring equinox is still six weeks away, with the idea of spring like a fine silver dust in the air that won't settle. There are very few signs of the season to be seen. But there are daffodils. Hundreds and hundreds of daffodils – or what will soon become them. The hard green spikes cluster in clumps every few feet and I feel a longing for their yellow faces. There are primroses too – their leaves, anyway. They look like wizened, crinkled palms pressing flat against the earth. The rest – the lesser celandine, the dead nettles, the garlic ramsons – are all waiting for the first undulations of chiffchaff song to kick-start them into action.

I duck under branches, jump a small brook, and then I see it. The reason I am in the woods today.

Peeling off my fingerless gloves, I reach out and place my whole palm on the trunk of my favourite tree. It is a coppiced alder with three thick branches parting ways from a single trunk, each branch a symbol of rebirth, determination and new life.

I've missed her.

Alder's life-giving properties are renowned across the Pagan community and its bark and small cones are often used to make healing charms. If you were to cut into an alder tree with a blade

– which I wouldn't advise doing, you monster – you would find your hands covered in blood. An alder is filled with a rust-coloured sap that looks incredibly similar to human blood. I think about the slow-moving resin oozing through the tree in front of me, it's life's blood cold and clotted in the winter air.

The cleft left between the coppiced trunk provides the perfect mossy sitting spot but I resist the urge to boost myself onto it today. It stands taller, broader, than the others around it and I wonder if this was the tree that inspired the wood to be planted – she is the Alder Mother with all her little birch babies fanning out around her, arms upstretched towards her crown. Under my bare hands, I feel the tree's familiar vibrating pulse – like a warm shimmer that I sense on the inside of my skin. It's something I have been doing for half my life – sensing the energy of things, expanding and contracting my consciousness by pushing it out from my chest, into the air just above my head then down the street and back again like a human-shaped yo-yo. Is this plant poisonous? Is this room a friendly one? Is this person a walking red flag? I've used this magical skill to cast my senses around a room like a net and sense for spirits or patches of dark energy. At home, even three years after her passing, I still feel my grandma standing next to me – her comforting presence and scent enveloping me when I need them most. I haven't been able to feel Sky but perhaps that will come in time or maybe I had never known what her true presence felt like and she is actually waving at me frantically, 'Here, Mummy, over here! Here! Why did I choose such a stupid woman to be my mum?'

This is not a skill I have always trusted and when I have chosen to ignore this ability – like when I heard a strong voice in my head that said, 'This person will ruin your life' but proceeded to befriend them anyway – things have gone very, very badly. Since then, I have always trusted my intuitive way of connecting to the pulse of people, animals, plants and stones; like sensing sweet, sour and bitter tastes with my tongue.

At least, I did a couple of years ago, before life became a little more complicated.

I wonder if I will still be able to communicate with the tree as I once did? Or is this intuitive magic gone from me forever?

When I was a teenager and first practising this trick, I didn't know how dangerous this could potentially be. If a consciousness, or soul, leaves the body, you are left open to something replacing that empty space within you; maybe a dark entity or a spirit just passing through. They say the soul weighs twenty-one grams – the weight of a shy and slinking mouse – and the brass scales must always remain in balance.

With a stuttering thought, I realise that had her soul still been in place when she was born, Sky would have weighed 621 grams. Imagine being so small that your soul makes up 3 per cent of your entire body mass.

In my mind's eye, I push away the flashback – one of the many that burst through unexpectedly. I need to exercise control. I can't let this keep happening outside of my bedroom.

Instead, I stretch out my senses to feel the alder's energy.

Under my fingers, the tree feels like the light on river ripples; like the dappled shade of the summer canopy. I feel the pressure of its energy like morning light through my eyelids. This tree is dreaming of brighter days just as much as I am. I smile and my dry bottom lip immediately splits open.

I've done it – I've felt into the tree's energy field – the first half of what I set out to do today. And it has been so easy! I know I should be elated to feel this little ember of magic and yet there is something hard in my chest. In my mind, I go back through all the times I've lain in bed staring at the ceiling, begging for Sky to come through and give me a feeling or just a few words that she is OK. If I'd been able to tap into the tree's energy so easily, shouldn't I be able to feel Sky around me? Or has she already crossed over, gone from me forever?

Crashing back to the task at hand and trying to feel encouraged by the energy I sense, I formulate the question I have come here to ask. I use my energy field to push my inner words outwards toward the tree:

'Are you happy to give me healing?'

I wait to feel the alder's answer.

Nothing.

Hmm. This isn't what communing with my favourite tree used to look like.

I remove my hands and frown. I focus on making my energy as calm and gentle as possible. Perhaps the alder is picking up on my prickly, dead-baby energy. I try again. Still nothing. Instead, I fumble for the tealight in my pocket – my small Imbolc light – and place it between the branches as part of the small ritual I want to perform. But the lighter is stiff in my equally stuck and cold fingers and, every time the wick does eventually catch, the wind whips through the cleft in the tree, leaving a smoking stump instead of a flame.

Hmm!

This isn't how I thought today would go. I'd come here to heal myself and to ask the goddess Brigid for a baby. But, no Imbolc fire, no baby. How very, very unblessed of me.

I take a deep, shaky breath and return my hands to the tree's trunk. I let my eyes roll downwards behind their taut lids, turning inwards and towards my palpitating heart. *Shush, calm down*, I think. *You are safe here, held by the Alder Mother. You are the baby now; let her hold you.* My own energy starts to hum a low vibration, like echolocation seeking out the reflected call of another life form. I am filled by a strong sense of being watched by something living but I keep my eyes firmly closed – I have heard no footsteps.

I ask again: 'Alder, are you happy to give me healing today?'

It doesn't come to me in words, but a feeling. A universal language. Faintly, like a moth's breath, the tree speaks to me by removing the firm shield of energy that keeps us as two separate beings, like a shift in the folds of a dress.

Yes, the tree tells me.

A thrill snakes through me, my diaphragm pushing upwards with joy. I did it! I can still do this. I can still speak with the trees. It hadn't been as easy as it normally was but maybe I wasn't so far away from my magic as I'd thought. I had reached out my consciousness and tapped the tree on its thorny shoulder as if saying, 'Hello. Do you want to play out today?' She has answered me like an old friend.

I'd like to think that a passer-by might feel embarrassed to have stumbled into such an intimate moment. But really, I know they'd just think I was off my rocker.

The alder tree merges its consciousness with mine and I am filled with a sense of calm. It comes in waves that glitter under my closed eyelids as if my conscious mind has been replaced with a shimmering orb of light. I hope the tree is also gaining from this exchange – gleaning wisdom from me about what it is like to see other trees than the ones in her rooted radius; fields of wildflowers; the sea.

In my stillness with the tree, I have completely forgotten where I am – something that hasn't happened in a very, very long time.

But then I hear it.

A panicked bleat of mourning sounds out like a shock wave. It sends a shiver down my spine and I feel the muscles around my eyes tense to pull back my eyelids in an animal reaction. The call sounds again – a worried, quivering cry of something wounded.

It is coming from the echoing expanse of moor beyond and my brain readjusts.

A curlew.

In February?

This is the earliest I have ever heard one. In winter, curlews stalk the winter coastline, returning to inland farms and grassland in early spring to breed and scare hikers with their wavering, eerie music. A creature with a strange curving beak, pieced together from odd parts, springs to mind as I stand frozen in the wood, listening. Its soul-pricking call of major and minor notes blasts ice through me while I lean forward against the alder tree. Out of sight but not earshot, the lanky bird plants its feet like an automaton – a ghastly imitation of a real bird – whistling for its mate in a ghostly 'come hither'.

They say it has been a mild winter, which accounts for the curlew's early return to skulk around for worms and frogs in the dead heather. But tell that to my heating bill.

My first death omen of the calendar year.

The first time I saw the UK's largest wading bird was over ten years ago – practically back in the mists of time – when my dad and I were birdwatching on the Wirral peninsula only a few miles from the coast. Stalking the perimeter of the mere with exaggerated steps, the winter curlew was on the prowl. Like the common heron, there is something prehistoric about the curlew: the way it moves in slow, meaningful strides through the wilted reeds; its precise steps heavy under the downward-curving beak. It is a creature so unlike us – but while its shocking appearance could inspire awe, there is something uncanny about its shape, its cry, its gait. You cannot look away once you have spotted a curlew. When I have seen them since, it has been in spring with a backdrop of yellow-green grasses and speckled moss, making them almost impossible to spot on the moors without a pair of binoculars or a scope. This lack of visibility is perhaps what makes them so rare in this day and age – who would want to protect what they cannot see? In Europe, the curlew is an amber-listed bird, given the status of 'declining' and, amongst a slew of environmental and habitat factors – with curlews often returning to the same nesting sites year after year, only to find them destroyed by JCBs – who would want to protect a bird so synonymous with death and mourning? W.B. Yeats knew this symbolism only too well:

> O, CURLEW, cry no more in the air,
> Or only to the water in the West;
> Because your crying brings to my mind
> Passion-dimmed eyes and long heavy hair
> That was shaken out over my breast:
> There is enough evil in the crying of wind.

In Celtic lore, the cry of the curlew is believed to signal the quickened approach of the Otherworld or the spirits of the deceased. After all, it does look like it just emerged from that second realm with a haunting message at the tip of its beak. In Ireland, its eerie call is believed to be a manifestation of the banshee's mourning cry – screaming out across the hills to foretell the death of a family member. The Cattle Raid of Cooley, the famous Irish myth, tells of the famed hero and demigod Cú Chulainn – son of the god Lugh – who fights a fierce warrior, the curlew-woman; a creature said to represent death itself. When Cuchulainn is victorious, it is seen as a triumph over mortality.

The magic of its mythological associations is also woven into the curlew's scientific name: *Numenius arquata*. *Numenius* means 'new moon', while *arquata* means 'archery bow', metamorphosing the curlew into the archer of the dark skies, its beak curving downwards to shoot sad, grief-tipped arrows to earth. With its cry, it herds the souls of those lost out on the moors, ready with its quiver to round them up at the gates of the Otherworld.

In spite of this, the curlew is also strongly linked with the coming of spring and the renewal of the land. Its call – due to its return inland at the first signs of warmer days – is said to herald the first licks of green into the world, putting it amongst the springtime ranks of the cuckoo and chiffchaff. Males create several shallow nest scrapes for females to choose from and, during incubation, both sexes add grass around the nest to help conceal it. Typically, the female lays four greenish, brown-speckled eggs arranged in a starlike formation with their narrow ends pointing inward to prevent them from rolling away. While both parents incubate the eggs, the larger female – identifiable by her longer bill – tends to take the dominant role while the off-duty bird remains nearby to issue warning calls. Both birds are on high alert due to the multitude of physical threats they face.

Recent research has highlighted another threat: hatching failure linked to eggshell quality. Studies[6] have revealed that thin, fragile shells – likely due to a dietary deficiency in the mother – may cause embryos to die in late development stages. Drawing parallels with similar issues in black-tailed godwits (also large wading birds), conservationists are now gathering shell samples from across the UK to better understand this phenomenon, an urgent undertaking considering the plummeting numbers of curlews across the UK.

I really do find it monumentally incredible how we have invested the time, energy and technology to study and understand the patterns and failings of birds and yet have nothing to explain much of the randomness of infertility and foetal abnormalities in humans. Despite the public outcry in women's spaces, maternal health and female reproductive systems have been vastly under-explored and underfunded, leading to chronic pain, mental health struggles and poorer physical health outcomes for an unfathomable number of women. Researchers saw the data that around 176 million women (around 10 per cent of all women) across the world have the debilitating condition endometriosis and decided to study the physical attractiveness of those with the disease, rather than ways to help their pain or understand the root cause.[7] Of course, when men suffer from a reproductive condition, things are different. Erectile dysfunction affects 19 per cent of men yet receives six times the amount of funding that research into pre-menstrual syndrome (PMS) does, despite the condition affecting 90 per cent of women.[8] It was only in the past two years that I – a grown woman – learned about how a mature human egg is literally shot out of the ovary as if by a catapult upon ovulation, to be caught dexterously in the arms of the fallopian tube. Surely, if prepubescent girls were taught how their bodies actually work, we would have approached our monthly cycles with wonder rather than just annoyance at their inconvenience? Similarly, research into the effects of recurrent miscarriage, foetal chromosomal abnormalities and pre-eclampsia is only just filtering into the public domain.[9] Newsflash: they are primarily caused by poor-quality male sperm rather than through any fault of the mother, despite most miscarriage testing still being performed on the mother rather than the father. The human urge to discover and share knowledge seems lacking in such key and vital areas.

For me, right now, the classic emblems of spring and the curlew are worlds apart. This duality of the curlew as both a spring and a death bird – a creature overseeing the most fertile, hopeful season, as well as the realms of the dead – is interesting, though. It is the yin and yang of the European countryside, the darkness in the light, the Persephone in Hades, and the calm before the storm because all that is born in spring is constantly fighting to survive and not everything will succeed.

Perhaps this was the most apt bird to hear on the festival of Imbolc – a time with one heel dug into the treacherous winter snows and its fingertips reaching towards spring.

I had spent my first years as a witch – back in 2002/2003 when glitter body gel and bootleg copies of Justin Timberlake's debut album were doing the rounds at my school – learning the meanings of runes, herbs and Tarot cards by rote, storing their mystical meanings into a velvet-clad portion of my brain. By grasping the properties and the symbolic meanings of these things, I could enhance my spell work and use this knowledge to predict the future. I learned the meanings behind dreams, trees, colours and even animals. The more mystical information I had, the more I could understand the hidden magic of the world.

And I could ward off any bad luck that was looming my way.

Over the years, I have made so many charms to protect me, wearing them around my neck or placing them in corners close to the door to keep evil at bay. But the rowan berry protection charm I'd bought for Sky's cot hadn't managed to smack away the sure and steady hand of Death.

So what did that mean?

From my forest glade with the alder standing tall in front of me, I feel as if the woods are protecting me like a talisman, hiding me from the curlew's view. But the glimmer of liquid magic I felt coursing around my body has now solidified into ice. My mouth tightens involuntarily.

What is the curlew searching for in the depths of the dead heather this early in the year? Who had its call been for? A mate yet to fly in from the coast? Or the one person in this wood who might interpret its cry?

Fate is a common belief within the Pagan community, which believes that our futures are laid out in the stars. Perhaps it is fate that I have heard the curlew today; a lament to death as I go about my mourning. What does it mean to have heard it at the festival of Imbolc, a time of renewal and looking ahead to the future? Perhaps more tears to come? More months of sadness?

But if this encounter was fated, what else was meant to be?

It is an uncomfortable thought. It makes my lips form a tight barrier over my teeth to stop myself from snarling. I squeeze my eyes shut, the tight, uncared-for skin of my forehead straining at the eyebrows.

My hands drop from the alder tree, our communication pierced by a curving bill. The alder – this symbol of strength, determination and courage – is so far away from me now.

'Thank you for your healing today. May you go in peace,' I say, in the kindest tones I can muster. It comes out as a monotone but I hope Mother Alder doesn't mind too much.

I grab my unused ritual candle then pick my way back through the muddy slicks on the path home again. Home to warmth, home to Linnet, and home to the smell of dirty dishes emanating from the kitchen.

I will try again tomorrow.

Chapter Five

Familiar

One morning, a few days after we got back from the hospital, I went in search of clothes. Our bedroom had quickly become a large pile of clean washing that 'I'll put away tomorrow', but I didn't head for that. I went straight to Will's duffel bag on the landing, the one we had taken with us to the hospital and that was still half-packed with socks, magazines and the 'emergency blanket' that would remind us of home amongst the sterility. I plunge my face inside. The bag itself smells like airports, crisped sandwich crumbs and old suede. But there is a rainbow-striped long-sleeved top at the bottom, one of mine, and I press my nose to it. There I catch what I am looking for.

Blood. The scent of blood.

Mine. Hers. Fated to be together.

It is the smell that permeated the hospital room forty-eight hours later, as no one bothered to clean up the splatter that had projected two metres from the bed. There had been no need to spruce up for loving family photos or balloon-wielding visitors, after all. It is the smell that still lingers in my nostrils and in my memory.

I breathe it in ever so deeply.

'At least you found out now and not at nine months,' was one of the most common things people told me in the beginning. And yes, that is true. At five and a half months, my bump could still be hidden under shirts and long, flowing dresses. At some points of the day, it's like it wasn't there at all. But first thing in the morning and last thing at night, it was round, hard and kicking. A live and pulsing half-moon.

Of course it is better to find out sooner rather than later that your baby is going to be in pain for her short, sharp life. However, I don't know how this particular feeling of loss could be bested in any way, shape or form. There is no 'at least'.

But some people go one step further. They say the five words that make my face harden and my soul retract:

'Everything happens for a reason.'

That's what a lot of people came out with in the weeks after her passing. They'd nod with a wisdom I had never seen in them before. They had the secrets of a sage, all of a sudden. *Everything happens for a reason.* 'Everything is a life lesson.'

From my years of witching, I'm friends with a lot of people in the spiritual community and this is a firmly held belief across the board. Before Sky, I believed this statement to be true too. The wheels of karma turn to distribute parcels of powdered doughnuts or hard-packed coal. Quick, you'd better choose whether you're naughty or nice this year, because good things come to those who deserve them. But, back in December when I looked down at the tiny coffin placed over mine and Will's knees in the back of the black limousine, I wasn't sure then and I am not sure now what I needed to learn. I'm not sure of the reason behind all this.

Do people not realise the weight of those words? As if Sky had done something to deserve being so sick. As if I had done something to deserve such devastating, life-altering grief. The New Age rhetoric reminds me: 'If only I had manifested harder that my baby would be healthy, then everything would be OK,' as if I could have done something to change this. As if it wasn't just two cells colliding at the wrong angle. As if it wasn't just a ripple in nature that changed our lives forever.

The NHS website says: 'Patau's Syndrome is a serious, rare genetic disorder caused by having an additional copy of chromosome 13 in some or all of the body's cells. It's also called Trisomy 13.'

Thirteen. An omen. Unlucky for some.

This rare disorder is what had given Sky her extra digits. It had also given her several life-altering defects, including a large hole in her heart, an echogenic bowel and a severely underdeveloped brain. She hadn't had a fighting chance and she would not have survived outside the calm safety of my body.

Before November 2023, I had never heard of Patau's Syndrome. It is rare but the condition affects one in every 4,000 babies, although the vast majority of these babies miscarry very early or die at birth so this number could be higher – we may never know. There are a number of characteristics that a Patau's baby might have, including several internal defects, but some babies may also have no eyes or recognisable facial features. The incredible midwife who delivered Sky had first come into the Butterfly Room with tears in her eyes. She had had the same experience as us when she was nineteen and had terminated her Patau's baby for medical reasons, as we had. The event was what had inspired her to become a midwife.

She went on to explain that the condition was 'not compatible with life'.

Patau's babies who do manage to survive the arduous birthing process are more likely to be girls, as female foetuses tend to be more robust, but the fact of the matter is that '[m]ore than 9 out of 10 children born with Patau's Syndrome die during the first year'. Those few who do survive are unlikely to ever walk or talk. That Sky managed to survive twenty-three weeks inside me is a miracle. Those kicks had been so strong; almost violent. Maybe, by another miracle, she would have survived the birth. Maybe. But if that was the case, I would most likely have had to watch her die in my arms shortly after.

A streak of madness flared in my mind repeatedly – both before and after the birth – and played its tricks on me. *What if they've got it wrong?* I thought. What if the scans I'd seen as I lay flat on my back with my dress hoicked up around my middle had been someone else's baby, Bluetoothed in from another room? A huge, sick practical joke. Or perhaps the doctors had secretly assessed me, classed me to be an unfit mother and were plotting to take my daughter away from me. These were all thoughts that snagged at my mind during that three-week period of waiting, hospital visits and near insanity. My risk factor of any chromosomal defects had been one in 5,000, one of the lowest numbers it is possible to have. How then could this be happening? It was only on seeing those little polydactyl toes in the delivery room that made me realise that maybe they'd got it right.

You never think it will happen to you. But she was the one in 5,000. This was happening to us.

Every website, forum and support group tells me some form of what is said on the NHS website: 'Patau's Syndrome happens by chance and is not caused by anything the parents have done. Most cases do not run in families (they're not inherited). They happen randomly during conception, when the sperm and egg combine and the foetus starts to develop.'[10]

Rationally, I know this. The condition, much like Down's Syndrome or Edward's Syndrome, occurs at conception when the cells mutate to hold extra chromosomes – in Sky's case, a duplicate of chromosome 13. It is random. Unlike the curlew's dietary deficiency, I couldn't have drunk another spinach smoothie or popped a few more folic acid tablets to prevent this. And yet, why does it feel like a thunderclap? Someone up on high pointing their finger from a far and distant cloud and uttering a fate that will change my life forever. Was this catastrophe fated to happen or is the Universe a vast and neutral space that can be influenced by karmic deeds?

'Everything happens for a reason.'

My mind flickers back to all the bad things I have ever done in my life. All the nasty thoughts. The shameful deeds that I could never tell a soul about except my diary in my most illegible handwriting.

My fault. Sky's death sentence was all my fault.

I did this.

Late February 2024
I am testing my boundaries. My world is still small and fragile. The first time I drove with Will a few weeks after the birth, I hit my front wheel into a roundabout and spent the rest of the journey in a state of apologetic catatonia.

But I need to keep trying.

You need to get moving, my mind tells me every time I look out the window. I'm absorbing books about PTSD, moving on from trauma and post-pregnancy nutrition, podcasts about Stoic philosophy and documentaries about how the mind has the ability to repair the body through the power of thought. I want to start healing – I am *determined* – even if my body feels like it's clunking and stalling a million miles behind where my mind wants to be. In fact, most of the time, everything from my hips to my toes is numb from sensation in a total trauma response.

Which probably isn't great.

It is a murky morning when I plunge down the twisting roads of Pendle. Each blind corner feels like it's on a forty-five-degree slope and my poor little Mazda Timothée relays his concerns in a series of whines and guttural grunts. His engine light has been on for six months and, even though the mechanic swears it's no big deal, there is a wince of panic in me any time I turn the ignition.

'You can do it, Timmy,' I say with a grimaced smile and a pat to the dashboard.

Will hadn't wanted to get up early so it was just me making this expedition today. He has been avoiding me most days but, then again, I guess I'm not great company at the moment. If only my trauma was more fun for my husband to be around.

After hearing the curlew, I had hoped that spring would be making an early guest appearance but the russet-coloured heather patterning every hillside and the brownish tinge to the low cloud lets me know we are about to reverse back into winter. On these angular bends and eye-flaring inclines, I'm glad the ice and snow predicted for this weekend haven't made their way to us yet. There has been enough horror in this part of the world. Here in Wonderful Witch Country.

This place on the very eastern borders of Lancashire was once full of those who could read the signs painted by the natural world; those who could interpret the smattering of starlings whooping and piping along the tree line, and the bloody spread of sheep entrails after a fox raid in the dead of night. In days gone by, Pendle was full of witches who ruffled the ears of their familiars – the Devil's sly and prickly messengers in animal form. Or so the records say.

A shudder of recognition floods through my body as I drive under the thick, cloying shadow of Pendle Hill and clock the hill's slanting shoulder, like that of an ancient goddess, tensed and poised ready to wrench herself from the earth if ever the people of her land are terrorised by witch finders again.

Here, I find it easy to see more than a grain of truth in those well-thumbed, seventeenth-century accusations.

I grew up on the story of the Pendle Witches; my childhood imagination was sustained by it. In fact, it was probably what started me out on my mossy ascent into Paganism. Ask any witch across the northwest of England about their first run-in with the craft and they are likely to regale you with tales of windswept moorland walks up Pendle Hill searching for any flicker of magic left over from the venomous 1612 witch trials that began here. Throughout the past eight years of my life, I've been slowly inching myself further north – drawn by the magnetic pull of the witchcraft Motherland. The area of Pendle lies almost smack-bang in the middle of the UK in northern England where Lancashire's green, rolling valleys upturn themselves into heather-twisted hills. Here, the carefully laid hawthorn hedges peter out and, instead, drystone walls weather the seasons, weaving together the landscape with rough, ragged stitches like the hastily sewn lining of a witch's poppet doll.

I have come here today mostly to get outside and feel like myself again. Now that my pelvic floor doesn't feel like it's about to make a run for it, this hiker needs to get her mopey thighs back in check and pull her brain out of the funeral parlour. I need to feel the wind on my face, I need to reconnect. Even though my eyes squint at the light.

But I am also here to be in the witchiest place I know and to hopefully feel the glint of magic tapping my collarbone. I have come to look for more positive signs, to shake off the curlew's haunting call. Maybe the magic that seems to have mostly deserted me will be twisted into a clutch of heather ready for me to tease it out. I'm sure the Pendle Witches would have known where to find those glimmers, so in tune with the land were they. Maybe I'll find some more hope in this familiar landscape.

I follow the metallic brown signs hosting white little witches on broomsticks, pointing you in the direction of where the coven might once have met. Felt-crafted hags hang in pub windows and every other shop has a witch's hat in its logo. It is all very jolly. It feels almost festive. But the reality behind the legendary tale is quite different.

While less known across the rest of the country, the 'discoverie' of witches in Lancashire was monumental. This was one of King James I's first chances to use his obsessive knowledge of 'demons' and fear of magic to eradicate a group of 'witches' and to set an example to other communities across the country. Occurring less than ten years into his politically tumultuous English reign, King James had already repealed the Elizabethan Witchcraft Act in 1604 and replaced it with An Act against Conjuration, Witchcraft and Dealing with Evil and Wicked Spirits, containing stricter punishments for those found to be performing acts of magic. He also republished his *Daemonologie* in which he claimed witches and witchcraft were running rampant around the country.

The words and ideals of the king, alongside the precarious religious politics of the time – where Catholics were actively sought out, imprisoned or killed for treason – put troubled thoughts into the minds of the god-fearing people of Britain.

So in 1612, Lancashire was alive with fright.

The undercurrent of fear led to the witchcraft accusations levelled against twelve people – mainly women – who were then tried at Lancaster Castle in 1612. Ten out of eleven (one perished in the squalid prison conditions) were sent to the gallows. All met with a grizzly end in front of crowds on the castle grounds after spending months in the worst conditions. Having visited the gaol at Lancaster Castle a few years ago, I know that the prisoners' fear still clings to the stones there; I could taste the metallic tang of panic in the air. Terrible things happened in those dungeons.

While the trials happened thirty miles away from Pendle in Lancaster, the Pendle Witches were rooted to this windswept land. Not only by their family names, which anchored them to the generations that had gone before, but by their animal familiars – their black dogs that prowled the land long after the condemned had left this plane. These large dog-like creatures were the omens of a lingering death and – for the people of Pendle – carried the smell of revenge between each yellowed canine, and the Devil's verses on their breath.

Although no witches reside in Pendle today, maybe their familiars were still here – one foot in this world and one in the next – and would recognise my grief, then come to greet me.

I pull on my crusty hiking boots in the car park and layer up. I know that the Lancashire weather can be changeable – to say the least. There have been times when I've had to abandon all thought of a climb as Pendle Hill has been lost in mist, its heavy outline completely invisible even up close. In his book *Pendle: Witch Country*, author and photographer Alastair Lee says:

> The area is exposed to some wild and spectacular weather which could easily be interpreted as a positive omen or equally an evil warning sign from higher beings or spiritual forces. When serendipity strikes and any given conditions just happen to follow a certain spell cast, we can start to understand how easy it was to believe in the power of witchcraft.[11]

But I am hopeful this time. I see a steady string of walkers far out in front of me looking like a spray of toffee wrappers in their bright hiking gear as they take the steep stone steps on the east side of the hill. I pick up my pace and add myself to the conga line.

Halfway up, panting and gasping, I realise how much time I've spent curled up with Linnet recently and – now that I've recovered some of my physical strength – I vow to tramp across moors, woodland and open fields all spring and summer long with my arms outstretched. However, this level of hope feels wrong in my chest – I am guilty of planning for the future and not living minute to minute like a true grieving person should. But I can't help it. A skylark whips up into the air to my left and my heart soars. I turn my face towards it. It is a grey speck in my peripheral vision but some primal part of me had been watching for the first signs of movement; for the first hint of longer spring-filled days. The bird sings its erratic trill as it disappears into the low-hanging mist – the feathers of its face slick with water vapour – searching for a mate perched on a cloud.

An old saying goes: 'Larks fly high when the weather is destined to stay fine.' But I look doubtfully at the sky.

I reach the top of the hill and am momentarily victorious. Out of puff but high up. Tall.

But my sense of joy over the wide open vista is short-lived as I switch my focus to swerving fell runners and dogs off the lead. I feel a swift pain in my chest, predicting all the skylark and curlew nests half-hidden in the grass that will be discovered by wet noses and errant hiking boots straying off the path this year. My sister works closely with local Pendle farmers as part of her job and is routinely told stories of leashless dogs savaging the grazing sheep that roam there. I am filled with horror at people's lack of consideration for the non-human world. It's a feeling that I have to tamp down in my chest every time I leave the house these days. The deep sadness I feel is for all those wild creatures trapped in a world they didn't make, want or evolve to live in. Their spaces are intruded on by all kinds of terrors:

by dogs of all sizes whose owners use the countryside as their personal playground, having little to no knowledge of what struggles to survive within it; by new motorway bypasses making remote areas readily accessible to thousands of people every day, giving wildlife less space to exist; by the light pollution that causes blackbirds and other thrushes to sing into the night and forgo their natural rhythms; or the noise pollution that causes chronic stress and fertility issues in animals and makes them forget their migration routes. The idea that everything designed to make human life easier and more efficient is destroying almost everything else's way of being gives me that feeling of body-breaking sadness I often feel I can't share with anyone. It is a feeling that on some days rivals my current state of grief.

I have been told this is a 'dramatic' way of thinking. But I'd say the twenty-first century is a pretty dramatic time to be alive, especially if you are a declining species laying your eggs in trampled tangles of heather.

Quick-stepping myself forward, away from the crowds of weekend wanderers, I force myself not to think of these things today. There is only so much a person is able to grieve at once before they implode.

The map crinkled in my hands is several years old and the carefully made path that spools out across the moorland to my right is unmarked on its pages. I fold the map away and forge ahead on this new route where the wind is less biting and stops whipping my hair into my eyes. I dip down to where the moor becomes marshland and, while I am thankful for the sturdy stone path that snakes in a jagged white line across the brown hilltop, the slippery slabs lead me to lose my foot in thick mud twice in the space of fifteen minutes.

This type of landscape might not seem so appealing to those used to golden fields and sapphire seas but there is a wild spirit to it that is wrapped around every exposed root and blackened, bent tree. It's a landscape that strips away the barrier between this world and the next – it is where you might expect will-o'-the-wisps; the spectres of those long-since lost in the bogs; and the clawed thorny feet of familiars as they traverse the land looking for hemlock flowers, foxglove pollen and other droplets of poison to spike their enemies with. Aside from the strongholds of ancient woodland, the moors are the place where I feel the pull of magic most keenly and hear those messages from across the veil – both the good and the bad. Perhaps it was also so for the seventeenth-century witches of Pendle, invoking the Devil in circles of gorse with the heather trodden down beneath their red peat-soled feet.

Think of a witch.

What is she wearing? A pointed hat and a long black dress, perhaps. What is she carrying? A broomstick and maybe a book of spells in the crook of her arm. What do you find at her feet?

If you answered anything other than a black cat or a toad, then I don't think we're on the same page.

It doesn't come as a surprise that most of us witches are animal lovers. As we know from the realm of TV witches and Halloween advertisements, witches are rather fond of a cat. Salem, Kit, Jiji, Crookshanks and Tabby are all magical feline companions lovingly named by their famous owners. Other familiars across history – in their various forms – also had cutesy and silly names: Tibb, Fancy, Dandy, Ball, Tom Vinegar, Jarmara, Pyewacket, Rug and Grizzel Greedigut. But these familiars were hardly witches' pets and the vast majority were definitely not cats.

The word 'familiar' began to be used widely in Europe during the sixteenth century but it seems to have first been reported in the witch trial of Dame Alice Kyteler in Ireland in 1324. Alice's familiar was a spirit that aided her magical workings and took the form of a man called Robin Artison, who was also her lover. At least this one wasn't an animal.

The term 'familiar' is derived from the Latin word *famulus*, meaning 'servant', a term that isn't restricted to animals, although that is most commonly how these familiars chose to show themselves (it was easier to stuff a rabbit into a cupboard if the authorities came by, after all). Familiars were said to be the Devil or his demons in disguise or a spirit (also called a 'familiar spirit') from the Otherworld with hidden knowledge that they would impart in a whisper to their chosen witch. A familiar would appear in a witch's home to help them do the Devil's bidding and perform a number of magical tasks, such as delivering a breech baby, diagnosing a mystery illness or healing a sick cow, before settling down to suckle their witch's blood through a teat hidden somewhere about her person. These familiars took on different shapes and guises depending on the person, with witch-trial records across Britain revealing familiars embodied in cats, dogs, hares, ferrets or toads – the slinking, slippery creatures that could sneak under your pillow or through the crack under your door.

This is certainly not the modern-day view of a witch's familiar – the soft-pawed cat at the end of our beds who sometimes stares into a flickering candle flame or an empty corner of a dark room as if absorbing occult intelligence. The Jacobean viewpoint was something much more sinister and completely believed by many. If you'd have spoken to any seventeenth-century judge, farmhand or milkmaid, they would have known to watch the animals for signs of the Devil – whether that be the Biblical hellraiser or the Pagan trickster Old Hornie. Both were just as dangerous.

Familiars in the burning days had a much darker purpose than scrounging scraps or keeping old women company. Amongst their misdeeds, familiars were known to sour milk – therefore damaging a person's livelihood and reputation – rot apples, urge witches to hurt children, commit murder and cause babies to be stillborn.

It was so much more convenient to blame the wise women, the misfits and the slinking familiars that prowled the streets after dark in search of their mistress's next victim. The beat of their paws sounded on the compacted mud tracks; the clank of their claws was heard on the milk churns in the yard just below your window. Reeling and stricken with mind-numbing grief, it is of course easier to blame the devil and his minions when a child dies, even though between the years of 1561 to 1700 in the nearby city of York, around a quarter of British children did not survive to reach their first birthday.[12]

My mind shuffles with uncomfortable, archaic beliefs of changeling children – how Sky's condition would have once been hushed away by legend, lore and magical thinking; how life was even more delicate in a world of midwives with muddied hands in the birthing room, and witches with spells of miscarriage and stillbirth on their lips.

Explained away by science, how might the Pendle Witches feel now, knowing their coven meets had been scrutinised and their curses debunked? How might I – a modern-day witch – feel to know that all the symbols I had always believed in were actually superstition? It is a bitter potion to swallow.

Real or not, the witch's animal familiars did not help them when they had the noose around their necks.

I've been walking a little while when I realise the traffic-light-coloured waterproofs around me have faded away. I am alone on the hill, which feels like a mountain, its edges completely out of sight. Scafell Pike, two hours up the road in the Lake District, is 978 metres high – almost double the height of Pendle (557 metres) – which is something else to behold, but I feel like I might as well be on another plane here on this mere hill. I look out over the twisted stubs of scrub and am met with silence.

Pure silence.

It is a sound I hear so infrequently that it shocks me into stillness. The wind has ducked out of earshot, folded into the earth. The mud has stopped its oozing. No skylarks call. I can't see any signs of life at all. The bracken is the deep brown of resting death and no smears of green show beneath its surface. Perhaps the fabled witches have spotted a kindred spirit in me and pulled me through a rift in time; another world where there is nothing except a deep, thrumming silence and a sense of gathering magic. In the stillness, this is a world that feels more alive than the real one I have just left behind.

AWEP-AWEP-AWEP-AWEP-A.

A male red grouse cackles behind me and blood begins to shoot through my veins at rapid fire.

I veer my binoculars over the tussocks, heart clamouring, until I find the bird with his scarlet eyebrows – also known as a wattle – laughing over the land from a rocky platform.

I watch him through the glass, my own breathing loud in my ears.

Maybe this is my own familiar. Had it come to tell me to make friends with my fellow hikers or chuck them over the edge of the hill (I hoped neither because I was feeling distinctly unsociable)?

The solitary grouse is often viewed as a spiritual symbol of spending time alone. When it is not trying to attract a mate, it prowls the moors in seclusion, blending its rounded brown body into the curves and crevices of the land, daring the world to leave it unseen. The bird is not heard until danger ventures too close, and then it lets out its eerie, manic laughter like a witch's cackle piercing the hills.

Alone though it may wish to be, it is my companion out on this misty ridge, occupying this liminal fairy space, out of earshot and out of time. If I were to scream, I wonder if the thick cloud around us would allow anyone else to hear me. There would only be the grouse to save me in this hollowed-out section of the hill.

This one won't be alone for long though. Red grouse males will soon be strutting their stuff for the less flamboyant females in late March to early April, calling their counterintuitive 'go back, go back, go back!' call, with females laying a clutch of six to ten eggs in a well-hidden scrape on the ground. Chicks hatch in early summer and will be fed by both the male and female until they are old enough to fly. Like a lot of ground-nesting birds, parents are often known for their theatrics, pretending to have broken wings to distract predators – both human and wild animal – away from their nests.

That's a skill they might need up here on the well-trodden Pendle Hill and goes to show the self-sacrifice that animal parents are willing to go through for their children.

I think about Will at home in bed and the air feels colder against my cheeks.

Was a grouse ever a witch's familiar, keeping her company from a watchful distance as she went begging along the upland paths? Sending her divine messages as she sat in solitude speaking with the land? It might not be a typical choice for a familiar but it is a bird so tied to this habitat, to the land the Pendle Witches carved their lives from, that maybe it was more than a fitting companion.

Out here on the moor, I seem to be looking for an animal companion that will guide my way, one filled with positive symbols and signs to use as a guiding light through my own dark night.

Maybe I am more lost than I realised.

This is something our ancestors have done throughout history, following the white stag through the forest in the hopes it will give them a message from the divine; feeding the robin in the garden to keep a passed loved one close. It is a way of controlling our immediate reality and making sense of a blown-apart world in the face of heartbreaking loss. It gives us hope that we are not alone but guided by a spirit who loves us from beyond the veil. Many say it is superstition, yes, but it is a tradition I am very happy to hold onto right now, even if it means trekking across the countryside until I can't feel my ankles anymore. Besides, maybe our ancestors knew more about the veil between the worlds than we do now.

I watch the grouse until it shuffles awkwardly out of my binoculars' range and I cannot find its comical expression again. It has become truly alone once again. I put one hand on my belly. Out on the moor with the wind whirling my hair in an uncanny circlet around my head, I too feel my aloneness. My loneliness.

If the grouse had a message, what was it trying to tell me? Maybe I need more time alone before I can get back to real life, despite the threat of unpaid bills and overdue book deadlines. 'Don't push yourself,' it says in a quavering, garbled voice. 'Take your time. Be alone, even if you are lonely.'

OK, Mr Grouse. Whatever you say.

He has a point, this omen of aloneness. In my grief, I'm certainly not ready to be fully back in the world again. I need more time.

But how much? Will there ever be a day in my life when I don't cry for her lost soul?

The rest of my day up on the hilltop is spent searching for safe footholds and crouching to slide down gullies on my bum. I swear I'm not always this ungainly but there is something about Pendle Hill that means my eyes are never on my feet – there is always so much to see. I am surprised to find a beck clefting the hill into a deep crag. I jump when I see a dipper curtseying over and over from below in the valley. A male stonechat displays his red breast to me from the other side of the stream before calling his flinty cry over the moor, and a wren stutters and starts somewhere out of sight in a tangle of bramble vines. It is still winter, but – away from the violent winds in this V-shaped dip – I can see why the birds are out and happy to be exploring nature again here.

I, too, am glad to be outside, occupying some ghostly semblance of my old self.

I reach the end of the path and debate retracing my steps, desperate for another two hours on the moor, but I see the bright curve of Ogden Reservoir ahead and know that a cup of tea, a veggie breakfast and the babble of civilised walkers carrying their witch souvenirs in paper bags are waiting for me.

Back home in the empty house, my legs aching and a hot water-bottle strapped to my chest, I tuck myself in on the sofa and hear the tell-tale jingle of Linnet's bell coming around the corner. Balance restored.

My face feels weather-battered but I already feel so removed from the windswept silence of the moor. I now have a phone full of signal; I click on my email app and drag down the screen, wondering if it will snag on any new messages while the susurrations of the dishwasher sound from the kitchen. As I got back behind my steering wheel, I could feel whatever wildness had attached itself to my skin being ripped away, trapped in the car door. It left a yearning ache in its stead that makes my skin feel raw. Perhaps that was just the icy cold or the knowing that it may be weeks before I get to return to somewhere as wild as Pendle again. My body feels sore, yes, but it's better than feeling hollow and numb. Maybe today really has started to shift some of that trauma that had lodged its heft between my hips. I poke my thigh hopefully.

Linnet hops up on the arm of the sofa with a soft '*Prrrrp?*' which translates to 'What a good girl I've been while you were away being weird on the moors, Mother. Is it time for a Dreamie?' So obvious, Linnet.

Linnet is perhaps the least mysterious cat in the world and wears her emotions plainly on her round little multi-coloured face. 'Oh, you want to stroke my tummy? DIE.' 'Oh, you want to feed me ten minutes later than my allotted teatime? I WILL SCREAM THIS HOUSE DOWN.' I remembered how when we'd first got her, she'd jumped up on the side of the bath, put her bum straight into a candle flame and singed her arse fur – a trick she's managed to repeat several times over the years.

'Oh, Linnet. You couldn't be a familiar even if you tried.'

She makes her way to my side and begins to settle down, resting her two front paws on my knee and slow-blinking up at me in a way that gives me a clear message.

'I love you too, Lin.'

She may not be my familiar but she always knows when she is needed.

Linnet turns her head upwards and begins to slow-blink at the corner of the room. I whip my own head around to the white ceiling. What or who had I expected to see there? Linnet is now looking at me, startled. 'That was for my eyes only, Mother. You'll see her again one day.'

I cast another look at the bare ceiling, hoping to catch a glimmer of light. Nothing. Linnet presses her paws into my leg with sudden urgency. What is she trying to tell me?

You are here. You are here. You are here.

The grouse told me I needed to find my strength in being alone, to rest and to not push myself back into society before I was ready. Hiding is sometimes good for healing. But I am never truly alone with Linnet at my side and I think that is a pretty OK loophole to take. Maybe Sky is even here too.

    Oh, cats. Whatever would we do without them?

Chapter Six

Fox

22nd December 2023
It is the Pagan festival of Yule but I have woken up long after dawn.

In years gone by, I would set my alarm early, intent on seeing the sun rise on this, the shortest day of the year. Today, there will be just seven hours, forty-nine minutes and forty-two seconds of daylight. In those past years, I would sit outside and watch the light turn the garden into a pale yellow mist, gently lifting the frost clasped around each blade of grass. I'd listen to the wrens in the misty scrub on the other side of the fence and look down to smile at Linnet as she wound herself around the legs of the garden chair.

But today is different.

Today is Sky's funeral.

I hadn't consciously chosen the solstice. When I had nodded to the funeral director, the significance of the date didn't even register – a time of magic and celebration across the Pagan world but the darkest day of the year, in more ways than one.

Will and I spend the morning sitting with Sky at the funeral home. Her small, white coffin is surrounded by fairy lights and a rabble of teddy bears donated by the funeral director's granddaughter. Inside the coffin, alongside her little body, I know they have placed the letters we have written to her, photos of us, a small white teddy bear and a knitted sky-blue heart. They are such small tokens and I wonder over and over again in my head on a loop if it was enough – if we could ever show her how much we loved her.

I had gone alone to the funeral home every night that week and every time it had got harder and harder to say goodbye; my coffin-side monologues had dried up in my throat, making me tail off mid-sentence and rest my forehead against the cool MDF to recover and breathe. I tried to tell her about us and our life stories so she would know all about her mum and dad. I even tried to read her *Harry Potter and the Philosopher's Stone* but didn't manage more than the first two pages.

I rasped with a half-smile: 'You'll have to come back if you want to hear the rest.'

This time – the last visit we will ever have – I press my thumb onto the butterfly inscribed on the silver plaque in the centre of her casket. I want to put my fingerprints all over it, tie strands of my hair to the handles, give her all the DNA and data her soul would need to find her way home to me when the time is right.

I realise then that I've gone a little mad.

Being 'mad with grief' is such an intangible phrase until you're glassy-eyed and there.

When we get back to the house, Linnet is suspicious. 'Mother, you are a dishevelled mess. Pull yourself together.' She narrows her eyes as we gather ourselves into an ensemble of dark clothes – the black feathers of mourning – then takes up her watch for the hearse on the folded mustard-coloured blanket on the window sill.

Three days after the birth, while my body was torn to shreds, one person – who shall remain nameless for their own safety – had asked me how I could be grieving so hard over Sky. About someone whom I had never met alive. Was I '...more upset about this than you were about your grandma dying – someone you knew for thirty years?'

Yes.

It is entirely different.

I have read somewhere that when you lose a baby, you aren't just losing them and their physical being, you are losing a multitude of possible futures. A tangle of paths we might have taken together. A lifetime of hopes that can no longer possibly come to fruition.

I knew everything it was possible to know about that little girl. I knew her sleeping patterns, her heartbeat, her most comfortable positions. I knew her birth time and her time of death; her star signs, her weight and all about her medical condition (my Google history is a testament to it). There was nothing else to possibly know about her except that she was my little girl. With a half-smile, I liked to tell people that she was always as good as gold because she never got a chance to do anything wrong.

And yet, of course, I thought about all the things that could have been.

I knew how I would have reacted to her first steps. The books I would have read to her in my grandma's old chair in the nursery. Where we would have taken her to watch birds, trains and the funny neighbourhood cats (I think she would have liked those best).

I tried to convey this in the eulogy I wrote, which Will reads to the small group of people gathered together in the chapel. No one has brought enough tissues for the amount of tears I cry but I nod furiously as Will reads out my words:

'Today is the winter solstice – the shortest day of the year. Which is exactly what you felt like to us. A short and dazzling burst of light that filled every edge of us with hope. Even though the day darkened once again.'

Afterwards, we listen to 'Bigger Than the Whole Sky' by Taylor Swift and I wilt into the lining of Will's suit jacket as the words hit my skin.

I kiss the coffin, the curtain closes and then we're outside again. Buffeted and blown by the late December storms. We are a cluster of crumpled black napkins next to the crematorium.

A crow caws and I wince. *We get the picture*, I want to scream at it.

I acknowledge how lucky we are to receive a funeral for a baby so young. Twenty-three weeks and three days. In years gone by, maybe even five years ago, we may not have been able to have a funeral for her. We might not have had the chance to say goodbye in the way that other people do. Her death and birth might have been hushed up. Forgotten by everyone except me and the dark linea nigra patterning my stomach.

Yes, I feel like we are the unluckiest parents who ever lived, but the funeral feels like an unexpected jigsaw piece of serendipity. Like catching a rainbow of light refracted onto the floor of an ambulance. We cling to our small, structured, public rituals with their familiar prayer patterns and colour schemes, as if they will contain us in soft-edged boxes when we are melting and falling apart.

But when I close my eyes, all I see is that coffin with its many symbols – the small, white flowers still tightly budded against the winter air, the silver butterflies, and my fingerprints pressed deeply into its surface.

25th March 2024
Throughout the grey weeks of winter, I had begun to understand the nature of grief.

I had the time to dedicate to it, after all. I had taken some extended time off my usual freelance writing work but maybe that hadn't been the right thing for my sombre head to do. Now I had long, unending blocks of minutes where my brain looped back through doctors' appointments, lying like a zombie in the maternity suite, and clutching Sky's memory box to me in the car on the way home like it was the greatest treasure known to humankind. Grief is slow; it is stony-faced. It is fur on your tongue and wearing the same jumper for weeks on end. Tears are your default state and any time not crying is spent with a face hard with salt. No wonder I looked like I'd aged ten years – I was being steadily eroded by the sea.

This grief state was certainly not something I had expected to experience in such a physical way. According to the NHS, the grey and grieving may have:

- sleep problems
- chest pain
- gastrointestinal issues

- increased risk of heart attack and suicide
- headaches or migraines
- heaviness in limbs
- aches in neck, back or skeletal joints
- muscular pain
- tiredness
- changes in appetite
- visual or sensory hallucinations

Even now, over three months on, I am going through more of these symptoms than I care to admit to my family, especially the scarier mental health symptoms that are worse in the mornings and evenings. But the fatigue has been the biggest shocker. I feel like I'm eighty years old and nap most days in front of the electric fire with Linnet on the back of the sofa behind me – my constant companion. I wake up disoriented, remember what has happened, then cry five tissues' worth of tears. I am confined to the house like a nineteenth-century TB victim; or – more likely – an hysteric. However, there are only so many days you can sit eating biscuits with *Gilmore Girls* and *Brooklyn 99* rolling on in the background before you start to look for patterns in the wallpaper.

Since the birth, I'd been in the habit of waking with a jolt in the middle of the night despite my earplugs' promise of a silent night. I'd be filled with the compulsion to lie straight as a bolt and listen intently to the house around me. At first I thought it was because I had heard a noise and was checking for intruders but then I realised that my brain was telling me to go and look for my baby. In her book *Matrescence: On the Metamorphosis of Pregnancy, Childbirth and Motherhood,* author and science journalist Lucy Jones writes about her own experience of pregnancy and the myriad mental and physical changes that happen in the mother or caregiver's body as they adapt to the needs of their child. Throughout the book, Jones describes matrescence as the momentous act of becoming a mother. Much as 'adolescence' transitions a person from childhood to adulthood, matrescence comes with its own physical, emotional and psychological challenges. Jones interviews neuroscientist Elseline Hoekzema, who co-led a landmark study which showed that pregnancy led to pronounced and lifelong changes in maternal brain structure that helped the mother adapt to the intricate needs of her child.

> The brains of the control group – who haven't borne children – are solely grey. But the brains of the mothers are dotted with pools of yellow-orange to indicate the regions that are structurally different. The coloured parts show areas of shrunken grey matter, in multiple brain regions. [...] [T]he lead author, Hoekzema, explained to me, volume loss can show a 'fine-tuning of connections'. Synaptic reorganization and fine-tuning, it is thought, make the brain more efficient and streamlined in what it needs to do to care for a baby.[13]

Despite having no living baby to care for, my brain had already been in the process of rewiring itself to become more alert to external dangers, to detect the first stirrings of small limbs before a feed and to predict the subtle changes of her facial features as she sought comfort from the sleepy warmth of my skin. My frontal and temporal cortices had changed forever to give me a new, hypervigilant identity that I wasn't living up to. I had no outlet for these recalibrated brain functions, with my mind constantly tricking me into hearing her ghost at two o'clock in the morning.

The first stage of grief is denial. The second is anger. The third is – oh, shut the fuck up.

It doesn't really work like that – they just tell you that to make it seem like the grieving process is something to be moved through logically and ticked off your to-do list. 'Ahh, I have reached the bargaining stage. Yippee, only two months to go before I get to acceptance.' Don't be fooled by anyone who tells you grieving is a linear process. I exist minute to minute, hoping to grasp onto a shimmering strand of happiness that will take me over the ridge into the next hour. A silly moment with Linnet; a tasty spoonful of jam; a family of long-tailed tits with their glittering calls on the bird feeder. But these shimmers don't come very frequently and they don't last long.

So, instead of feeling motion sick from my pinball grief journey, I am taking the grouse's advice. Sitting; being still. But if I'm honest with myself, I am not resting – I am lolling and generally being as useless as it is possible to be. My head is urging me to 'heal, goddamn you, heal – move on!' but my body is sluggish and in need of oiling around the hips. The trip to Pendle absolutely wiped me out. This had been a hike I'd done a dozen times before in a landscape I knew well but I'm dizzy, shaky and knackered even weeks later. Surely this can't be a typical part of grief? I've heard of people returning to the office a fortnight after their own mum had died. How could they possibly manage that when I am still rotting here three months on? I am not used to sitting this still and I feel the confines of my cosy living room like a padlocked coop. At this time in any 'normal' year, I would be solo hiking across the West Yorkshire moors, a good audiobook yammering away at 1.75 speed in my earphones and trying to ignore the ice chunks crunching dangerously below my feet. But the physical side effects of grief have startled me into submission.

Right now, there is nothing I can do to speed my journey along. I have to sit with this. The grouse said so. But, my goddess:

I. Am. So. Bored. Of. It.

Spring is announced with the peeps and trills of pre-dawn robin song, and something stiff and dark begins to uncoil in my chest. The furled hand of winter, ruled by the Crone goddess Cerridwen, fully releases, letting me go, swearing she'll come back for me next year – although I really wish she wouldn't.

The first few days of the season offer no glimpse of green. My heated mattress topper is still blasting all night long but perhaps that's the price you pay for living in the northern hills, where we are often snowed in until the last weeks of March.

But I can smell the fresh live shoots in the air and feel them cutting my bones with veins of chlorophyll.

The spring equinox occurs every year when day and night balance perfectly. It is the solar reawakening of the hemisphere when light slowly begins to fill the cup of the year until she brims all the way to the top at midsummer. In some areas of the Pagan community, the equinox has been renamed as Ostara, linking the festival to the goddess Eostre, the root of which also gives us Easter and oestrogen. Many people believe both the festival and the deity have been passed down through the centuries – however, Ostara is actually a very modern term, first coming into common usage in the 1970s with little to nothing being known about the goddess Eostre at all.

Cybele, however, is an ancient spring deity. She is a very early Roman mother goddess associated with nature, fertility, healing, protection, motherhood and agriculture. Although nurturing in her demeanour, Cybele isn't like the calm and gentle mother goddesses we know from other pantheons: she is wild – a lioness protecting her cub – and will go to extreme lengths to keep her followers safe. As a goddess linked with spring, we can see her as a fearsome force, hell-bent on keeping her seedlings and loved ones away from harm. Every spring, a festival used to be held in her honour – with her large procession of followers going to extreme lengths to prove their devotion to her. The cult of Cybele was extremely popular and people would whip themselves into a frenzy – quite literally – practising self-flagellation to show their devotion to the Great Mother and ask for her blessing, protection and good health. Thankfully, you'll be pleased to hear, this practice has died out and we can now worship the brighter days in less painful ways.

This is a different kind of spring for me, as with the new season comes Mother's Day and then the date I've been dreading most of all.

Sunday, 31st March. Easter Sunday. My due date.

This is the day I should have been preparing my home and my life for. 'Don't forget the car seat,' I'd bark at Will, clutching my lower back like a pregnancy parody. But instead, I am just preparing myself mentally, steeling myself against the bite of this calendar date. I am now faced with a surplus of time that stretches out before me like a dirt-covered yellow-brick road. This was not time I was supposed to have. I was supposed to be preparing for night feeds right now. Or exhausted trawls around the park. When, in fact, I'm suspiciously well-rested. This is a season Sky will never live through; I am supposed to be showing her all this wonder right now. She is supposed to be here.

Because of this, I feel more than a little desperate: desperate to go outside, desperate to be feeling better already and desperate to know when I might have another baby. My powerless frustration rumbles through the house. Over the past few weeks, I have consulted three different mediums and each one has given me a different date for when I will get pregnant again. I have had Tarot readings and shamanic healings while I sit numbly waiting for divine advice. Each reading has been... not very positive. In spite of this, I am determined to get answers. I am desperate for a sign.

So we decide to get away from it all.

Will and I leave for a long weekend to Whitby on the northeast coast over Sky's due date. We've booked a small cottage in a hamlet in the North Riding Forest Park. All around us, Dalby Forest sprawls out; its evergreens needling the air with the fresh, sharp scent of life. Despite being seen as a winter emblem, pines are a tree that actually symbolise life itself. Followers of the Greek god Dionysus carried a *thyrsus*, a (rather phallic) staff topped with a pine cone and wrapped in ivy, symbolising fertility and prosperity, and druids back here in Britain would light large bonfires of Scots pine at the winter solstice to draw back the sun's lifeforce.

We arrive at the cottage, light the fire and sit with the sounds of the wind howling around the stone.

This is the first time I have felt true peace in months. No languishing, just calm.

Away from the daily sights of my grief and Sky's urn on the mantelpiece, my breathing feels deeper and I have a sudden burst of energy.

'I'm going to go and explore,' I announce, shoving on my filthy boots. 'Do you want to come?'

Will ducks and looks dubiously out the window. 'It's getting dark though?'

'I just need to go and stretch my legs; I'll be back really quick.'

Over the past few days, the local Facebook groups of northern England had hushed their chatter about road works and dog poo and had banded together to rejoice in a rumour that the aurora borealis was visible across the moors and dales. Practically fizzing with excitement, I'm hoping this luck will spill over into another chilly day. We are staying close to a Dark Sky Reserve, a place so remote and unpolluted that you can see the Milky Way, so I'm ready to jump on this 'astro-tourism' and try my chances.

The evening sky holds a pink and lilac shimmer, which I hope is some fairy-like foreshadowing of the aurora but is more likely just the effects of the early sunset. Armed with my Ordnance Survey app and a scarf, I plunge into the countryside down a steep bank into a green valley. Where I promptly lose phone and internet signal.

All around me is deathly quiet.

I realise immediately that the area is so unpolluted by light because there isn't a human soul for several miles around – of course. I think of Will back in the cottage, snarfling bits of cheese in the kitchen and roasting his toes by the fire. No way of contacting him now.

I smile to myself at my own recklessness but the route is only short and I'm sure it will be easy to follow...

Ten minutes later, I'm in ankle-deep mud at the bottom of the valley. The River Derwent has burst its banks and has created an oozing pool of mud around the bases of the trees. It squelches into the ridges of my hiking boots, creating a new coating that I'll probably never wash off. The path is... this way, somewhere, if it decides to materialise again. A wispy crescent moon appears as I continue to wade precariously close to the water's edge. In the space of ten minutes, the sky had darkened to indigo, then a deep sumptuous blue, revealing the North Star.

I am nowhere near the path and nowhere near the cottage.

What a stupid idea this was.

As I turn to where some pained spirit guide is pointing me, I realise that there is a stillness in the air like on a hot July evening rather than a gloved March night. No birds call. No tree moves except for the vibration of light rain as it drops through the leaves. My stomach flips.

I know I am being watched.

A movement catches my eye about fifteen feet over my shoulder.

A gliding shape emerging from the tree line.

A watchful ghost. A fox.

In the blue twilight, its coat looks grey, as if its Arctic cousin has rolled in soot.

The fox is stock-still, its back legs in the greenery and its tail bristled like a cat's. I am so still that the blood in my veins is forced to slow to a trickle.

In the half-light, I can barely make out his eyes. Perhaps they are bleary with hunger; consumed by it. Or maybe just mildly curious. 'Ah, another Two-Legged on my patch,' it thinks as I stand bundled in my winter coat and gloves, incapable of heating myself, feeding myself... defending myself.

I think, with a pang, of how the lengthening days will soon mean much shorter hunting hours for the fox. The air will be alive with the scent of blossom and bluebells. Perhaps this crepuscular creature is stocking up while it still has more of a chance of catching the rich, fleshy scent of whatever he can snatch. But on the flipside, the coming mating season will mean an abundance of young, love-drunk voles, mice and rabbits, which will make pickings easier.

Perhaps this one is hunting to keep its mate fed; a batch of four little cubs still nestled in her belly inside their den. When they are ready to be born in a few weeks' time, throughout April and May, the male will deposit food parcels – meaty care packages – at the entrance of the den for the female to take tenderly between her teeth and drag inside. I feel a pang of jealousy and incredulity over the fact that I am envious of a fox that I've made up in my head.

Red fox mothers, or vixens, have a relatively short gestation period of around fifty-two days, unlike other canids, such as domestic dogs or African wild dogs, which have longer pregnancies. The vixen's quick reproductive cycle ensures cubs are born early in the year, giving them ample time to grow and develop before winter.

Pregnancy is a delicate time for the fox – whose life of dodging traps and farmers is already precarious – and not all embryos survive. Studies have shown that some are reabsorbed into the mother's body if conditions are not optimal. Despite these losses, vixens often give birth to four to eight cubs, although cases of up to thirteen have been recorded.

As birth approaches, the vixen seeks a safe and secluded den – known as a natal earth – to raise her young, digging new dens each year or repurposing old ones, often choosing locations beneath sheds, outbuildings or even gravestones. The deep bond between the vixen and her mate ensures she keeps well-nourished as she prepares for the demanding weeks ahead.

When labour begins, the vixen remains within the safety of her den to give birth at night. The mother licks each cub clean and makes sure they are warm and safe. In those first two weeks after birth, the vixen is almost constantly with her cubs, rarely leaving the den except for brief moments to relieve herself. This is a critical period, as the cubs are blind, deaf and utterly dependent on their mother's warmth and milk for survival. The vixen depends entirely on the dog fox to keep her and her cubs alive.

The cubs grow and the mother gradually spends more time outside the den, though she remains fiercely protective. The first time the father sees his offspring is usually when they begin emerging from the den at around four weeks old. Even then, he maintains his role as a provider, leaving food near the den entrance while the vixen continues to nurse and guard the cubs.

As this dog fox passes the many winter months alone until it can finally clap eyes on its young, is it also being driven half mad by hope?

By day, Dalby Forest swarms with families and dogs, pushing nature back into the margins despite the healthy show of greenery the area has on offer. I wonder where a fox's den might actually be in this usually touristy place; where its cubs might be born. Between 70 and 80 per cent of fox cubs will die before they reach maturity, which perhaps accounts for the haunted look in the fox's eye.[14] Some will never leave the safety of the den, taken by disease before their time. Others will fall prey to natural predators and cars. More, as we know too well in the UK, will be caught up in the Hunt. There is so much to contend with and this fox's life is thanks to its own wiliness.

Perhaps this fox has walked many miles in search of a meal. Perhaps it is just incredibly good at lying low during the day.

He is just trying to survive.

I flick my eyes away to the path, looking for anyone coming this way, worried that any newcomer might frighten the fox away or might frighten me. But in that single second outside of my gaze, the creature sees its opportunity. It employs its ghostly powers to 'fade away into the forest dim'.

The fox has gone, with the soundlessness of an apparition.

I am left with only the sound of my own breath and the rush of the moonlit river. A cow's rolling moo calls in the distance so that I know the vision is over. Had my encounter been a glimpse of the darkness or something else?

The fox doesn't feel like a happy symbol to see out on a cold March night. It is one of survival and scrappiness. It is saying, 'At least we're alive.' And that is pretty much all I can say for myself as well.

Darkness is falling rapidly around me and my heart begins to pucker more quickly in my chest. I am in the valley's basin and have a steep scrabble ahead of me.

I take a right turn and end up in a swamp that would rival the Dead Marshes. Wading to the valley's edge, I find a foothold that will begin taking me upwards. I think.

The climb is beyond steep and I am bent double when I see the reassuring headlights of a road up ahead. I've made it; Will won't have to spend the evening talking to the police after all.

I hear a guttural *YAT* in the undergrowth behind me and I run the last quarter of a mile back to the cottage, jumping over tree roots, feeling the fox's keen eyes on my shins.

It's easy to see why foxes have been depicted as villains across time.

Their blasting screams are something less akin to a bird screech and more to an actual demon. While once you might only have been jolted awake in the middle of the night if you lived on the edge of wood or moorland, now foxes are close enough to the human world to spark children's nightmares on almost any suburban street. Their physical appearance alone may make you think of Sly Mister Fox before *Fantastic Mr Fox* springs to mind. In literature and film, if someone is described as an 'old fox' or has 'vulpine' features – a pointed face and a canny smile – they are almost always doing someone dirty, usually stealing your life partner *and* your millions at the same time.

While they might not have the mistrusted death feathers of the corvid family, the fox's russet coats have become synonymous with deception. It has been this way since the medieval period at least.

In the twelfth century, the 'Reynard Cycle' was a popular collection of stories centred around the adventures of slippery Reynard the Fox. In the stories, Reynard is an anthropomorphic fox who uses his intelligence and cunning to outwit his opponents, overthrow social hierarchies and escape tricky situations. The main message behind the tales was something like, 'Hey kids, watch out for those foxy characters who'd rather trip you into a cow pat than dob themselves in.'

This message has persisted in popular culture in children's book characters (teach them young) such as Beatrix Potter's Mr Tod and Foxy Loxy in the folktale 'Chicken Little'. But to get a clearer sense of the public opinion of foxes, you only have to look as far as their collective name. A group of foxes is called a 'skulk'.

A skulk. Nasty little lurkers with a trick up their sleeve.

On top of this, foxes are commonly seen as pests, known for their love of lambs and domestic fowl on farms and smallholdings. Methods of fox killing over the years have included such 'humane' ways as poisoning, shooting, trapping, snaring and gassing.

However, this bad feeling often goes one step further. In earlier times, foxes were sometimes considered to be evil:

> In early Christian and medieval thought the fox was considered to be a demonic animal. The tendency in Greek and Roman tradition to attribute a negative significance to the animal was taken up and further developed. The fox is a symbol of the devil, an image of demons, and because of its slyness and cunning it characterises both the ruler who does not fear god [...] and a cunning person in general...[15]

But, as is so often the case, the animals who were demonised by Christianity were revered by those who came before them.

In Celtic lore, foxes are depicted as spirit guides – the walkers of two worlds – appearing to ragged travellers in the snow-hushed wood to pass on hidden wisdom and divine guidance from the other side.

The fox was also beloved of the Irish goddess Brigid, ruler of the festival of Imbolc and of spring. Cunning, intelligence and wisdom in Irish lore are all seen as positive traits and were often linked with Tuatha de Danann – the magical and revered race of fairy folk found across Eire – with the fox seen as their earthly counterpart, distributing their wisdom to those who sought it above ground. If you spotted a fiery red pelt trotting your way over the hillside, you could be sure some mind-bending news was about to be revealed.

This is a more positive way of viewing the fox. In Robin Page's book *A Fox's Tale*, he explains how a hunted fox's brush would sometimes be hung above a stable door to ward off evil and bring good fortune. Plenty of benefits for humans; however, none at all for the fox. This duality also plays out in Native American legends, where some foxes are seen as wise and benevolent, helping those in need. Other times, he is a bad omen and a greedy thief – a permanent outsider in search of a chip shop wheelie bin.

But which of these many messages had my fox been trying to convey? We had been so alone together – I'd been all ears.

I think about the times I have come across foxes in my life and remember the eerie quiet and stillness that accompanied those apparitions; their noiselessness helping them walk the line between the veils of this world with masterful footwork. Aside from the barn owl, they are the ghosts of the animal world, carrying fairy news on their translucent hackles. But – oh – they are also beautiful creatures; there is absolutely no denying it. Playful in their autumn colours, the falling light glinting off their russet coats; their bright colour is unmatched across so many landscapes. Perhaps they are alone, cutting a striking figure across the misty fields in their tattered scarlet jacket, or they are surrounded by a litter of blue-eyed cubs tumbling over one another with yips of delight. Either way, they are radiant; the muse of the wildlife photographer and a coveted sight on any country walk.

What if the ongoing media onslaught of negativity about foxes and the vitriol from farmers, gamekeepers and the elite was just humanity's fear of the messages that the fox brings from beyond this world?

What if the fox's message was one of hope rather than fear?

The 31st arrives.

I wake up and take a deep breath that fills my entire body. The exhale is more than a little ragged.

My plan today is to spend her due date with Will overlooking the North Sea, where the sky is at her most magnificent. I want to tell my daughter how much I adore her and miss her while gazing out at the horizon.

But the day is cold and dreary; a perfect colour-match for my mood.

Will is asleep but I can't stay in bed. I want to *do* something. I need to be moving. I haven't tried to do any magic since my failed Imbolc ritual but I am feeling the tug of witchcraft at my wrists.

Witchcraft is a grounding constant in my life and if I'd learned anything from writing *The Wheel* it was that I could always return to it no matter how long I'd been away from my path. Right now in my life, everything else had gone tits up and I was in the process of questioning everything I'd ever known about the world. But if I removed witchcraft from the mix too, who would I be without it?

I shower and head out to the garden to cast my circle.

The cottage garden overlooks a large valley that catches the dawn light. Two buzzards circle at eye height over the trees and I begin to steady my breath, turning inwards to gather myself into calmness.

I don't have many tools with me but I light a white candle in a south-facing spot and call in the Four Elements.

'Hail to the Guardians of the North. By the powers of Earth and stability, I invoke thee, I invoke thee, I invoke thee. Hail and welcome.'

I then repeat this for the other Elements – Air, Fire and Water – and begin to invoke the goddess of this time of year.

'Brigid, I welcome you into my circle. Lend me your energy to heal myself in troubled times and bring me your peace and light. I invoke thee, I invoke thee, I invoke thee. Hail and welcome.'

The trees around me ripple in the light spring breeze. In past rituals, the goddess herself has stepped into my circle in real, touchable, corporeal form. While this isn't the case today and I doubted my inner magic was strong enough to make any big invocations, I know her signature and can feel her presence. There is a shift in the energy around me and I feel a lightness enter the circle as if a being made of pure brightness has illuminated the space.

Hello, Brigid.

It is time for the ritual to begin.

I sit cross-legged on the patio and stare into the shuddering flame of the white candle. This time, it stays alight.

'Dear Goddess Brigid, I want you to help me heal my trauma and grief. Please take it from me and replace this sadness with light. I am doing all that I can to bring this change into my life; I am writing about what happened, I am speaking about it with friends, trying to move my body and really trying to find positive moments. I am willing to try anything I can to feel better. Please can you give me the extra boost of energy I need to keep healing and moving forward with my life?'

I am met with a dull silence – only the faint buzzard's cry sounds in the misty valley. I grimace into the candle flame. Hopefully, I'm just not picking up Brigid's signs.

I raise my arms and say to the flame:
'Goddess Brigid, come to me in my time of need,
I am ready to serve you and I am ready to heal.
On this morning, I light a sacred flame,
I ask you to take my sickness and help it wane.
Alleviate my trauma and grief to help me thrive,
help me feel healthy, renewed and alive.
Brigid, goddess of rebirth, fire and the forge,
burn through the old ways and help me transform.'

Pushing my cold bum off the flags, I start to move around the circle three times in a clockwise motion. I walk in a stately fashion but maybe the spring goddess would prefer it if I leapt around like a fawn. I'm not feeling especially frolicky today so she'll have to make do with a reverent pace. When I have completed my three circles, I sit back down in front of the candle flame and allow myself to drift into a meditation.

Do I feel Brigid near me? Not as strongly as I have done in the past – her distinctive girlish energy isn't eagerly around me like before – but there is a sense of clarity to the circle. I feel like I've been heard.

'Thank you, Brigid. I don't have an offering to give you today but thank you for everything.'

'What are you doing?'

I turn around and see Will's head emerging bleary-eyed from the bedroom window.

'Just telling the Goddess Brigid to transmute my pain into healing.'

'That's very on-brand of you.'

'Want to ask her anything?'

'No, but I'll come sit with you. Give me a sec.'

I blow out the candle and uninvoke the Elements and the goddess while I wait for Will to come out with two steaming mugs of tea.

The cloud is low over the valley and the sky isn't showing itself at all but now seems like the right time to say what I have been meaning to say. I take a sip of tea and speak out loud while Will looks solemnly at the ground.

'Sky, it's Mummy and Daddy. Today is your due date and we are pretty sad down here because we want you to be with us so much. We know you should be with us right now and we are so, so sorry that you're not. Please know that we love you so very much.'

They are words I've said five hundred times but they are all I can manage as the tears choke me up for the tenth time today.

'Come back to us soon.'

Like the fox, I am speaking to those beyond the veil. I am ragged but alive.

Just about.

Chapter Seven

Augury

Nostalgia can help to cover the cracks left by grief.

My due date has sparked a new wave of sadness in me and I begin to long for the things of my past when I still had no knowledge of life whatsoever. Just the feel of plastic toys beneath my fingers and juicy green lines under my nails from making daisy chains.

I want to be nowhere else in the world except my grandparents' kitchen table, eating Lurpak on toast and playing Scrabble with my grandma. The urge comes over me in an almost violent attack of longing. My grandparents had been dairy farmers and owned the oldest house in our village – a creaky, vine-covered, gothic-novel dream – with the dairy in its grounds. In the '60s, however, they had decided to tear down the house, which had been doing a good job of tearing itself down since its foundations got rattled in the Second World War. So I had only ever known the spacious dormer bungalow and sprawling green lawn they replaced it with. The garden was where I had collected the hard knots of fallen unripe pears and had first shown an interest in birdwatching. Grandad and I would stand at the window of the playroom, knees against the radiator, and watch the green finches, blue tits and the noisy jays through his comically huge pair of binoculars. The highlight of the year was always when the wrens – who nested religiously in the wall of ivy that bordered the whole left side of the garden – had their first brood and turned the ivy into a shivering, tweeting grotto. Seven-year-old me would wonder how many wrinkled pink babies with bulging eyes craned their heads upwards inside the tangle of leaves. If you looked away from the wall for a few moments, you'd miss the little ping-pong ball of feathers propelling itself out of the nest to begin its distinctive clockwork call on the other side of the garden. My grandad, in his wellies and green canvas gardening hat, would say, 'Just like you, little Jenny Wren.' I never could sit still.

I am craving this safety. I want nothing more than to open my eyes and be in that warm, wood-panelled kitchen with the smell of the summer sun scorching the tablecloth and roast potatoes crisping in the oven.

When my grandma passed away in September 2021, in the midst of the devastation, I had taken a few things of sentimental value from her house: the brass wind chimes that had hung in the hall at the foot of the stairs, the turquoise glass vases that had sat on the dining room window sill, a stout antique bookcase and, most important to me, a small porcelain doll that – when wound up – would play the theme to *Love Story*. As a child, I had loved to wind up this doll – the Green Lady: a russet-haired woman sitting in a long green dress and holding a dove in her outstretched hand – and hear her music tinkling all through the house.

When I brought her home, I put her in the spare room. But there, she started misbehaving.

Whenever important dates would occur, the doll would have something to say about it. The Green Lady successfully predicted the conception of my niece by playing her pretty little tune in a silent room after not being touched for months.

Ding ding ding-ding ding.

Sixteen months on, she had predicted Sky's conception too, singing her song just three days before I tested positive.

On the day of Sky's funeral, five minutes before the hearse arrived, Grandma's Green Lady was at it again.

Ding ding ding-ding ding.

My face went white with shock and I immediately screamed for Will at the top of my lungs; the magic of it transported me to the realm of spirits, calling for my attention.

But then I'm back at my own dining room table, unwashed and shaking. My grandparents are gone too and I wish with all my might they could tell me that they're with Sky and that she's safe. Now, the Lady is still and eerily silent on top of the tall bookcase. On the longest of my days, I glare at her, willing her to play those first tinkling notes.

Grief goes in circles. Everything goes around and around until I am motion sick with the constant movement. The writer Max Porter said grief is 'the thing with feathers'. Abraham Lincoln called it 'a sad sweet feeling'. To C.S. Lewis, it was akin to fear. But I have found it to be a cracked and rusted fairground carousel; one that is difficult to disembark from.

It jerks me in one direction – towards the image of my daughter's still, sleeping face – then lurches me over to a single magpie with its open mouth held skyward.

I have been going around and around on this merry-go-round for so long that I start to wonder if it's all a dream. If I slap myself in the face, I will wake up, look down and see the arch of my belly rising under the sheets. I'll put a hand there and feel her tiny, slender feet dimpling my palms.

By the time I've felt the relief of this idea, I'm knocked back into the centre of the carousel. Round and round we go.

Small feet. Tiny hands. A white coffin. Small feet. Tiny hands. A white coffin.

Instead, to occupy my mind out of sight from Will, I google Patau's Syndrome and look for people sharing their stories. This might not be a good use of my time but I do so nonetheless with an obsessive glint in my eye that fixes me to the screen for hours at a time. I come across a website that gives me the names of several tiny Patau's babies and how long they lived outside of the womb. Ten weeks. Three days. An hour and a half. Seventeen minutes. Will would, quite rightly, smack my phone out of my hands if he saw me looking at these things. 'Don't do this to yourself,' he'd say. 'You're only making yourself upset.'

And I am. I'm doing it to myself. I want to feel the pain of it, because how else will she know how much I'm suffering? How I think about her two hundred times a day, even when I'm grinning for a photo on a hike, blasting '90s classics down the M62, spearing summer rolls at my best friend's birthday meal, packing for a minibreak? How else will she know how guilty I feel?

If you looked at me, you'd think I was fine. But it's a lie.

Look closer and you'll find the underside of my skin is coated with glossy, black feathers. These underwings prickle and long to burst through the skin and fan themselves out, to luxuriate in their iridescent splendour. I'm just hiding them well under long sleeves and a smile.

In my darkest moments, I whisper, 'I wish it had been me instead.'

'Hello, my darlings,' a voice like velvet croons from my laptop. 'How are we all this evening?'

I sit up straighter and lock my eyes on the screen in front of me.

The days are growing longer, leaving no excuse for eight p.m. bedtimes. But I'm finding now that I need to sleep less; the physical effects of grief are draining out of my body and I want to raise a glass to Brigid for tipping all that inner sludge down the drain. The power of ritual work coupled with the spring daylight is a thick and healing elixir, even if it has only been for the physical side of things. In the evenings now, I head out to the fields to see the flurries of blackthorn blossom and catch the pale lilacs and clashing golds of the sunset. With spring's fresh light, I feel like I can observe the world's beauty without the sense of guilt that I had before – I am allowed to glance at pretty things other than her face.

Right?

'You look so much brighter,' says Will with a hint of encouragement. I can't tell if he's outright lying to me but there is something different about April. My face doesn't quite look like me again, but I catch myself reflected in a car window as I walk up a country lane and quite like the colour of my skin against the background of green. That green pulse is returning in me – along with some well-needed body weight. The land throws out wisps of living birdsong that I catch on the air, half-remembering what it was like to thrive and want and dream, rather than just survive. The bluebells will be out soon. I picture their worm-like shoots cracking the hard outer casing of the bulb, pushing through the spring-showered soil in search of light but not quite finding it. Almost, but not just yet.

I'm coming back to myself.

Although I am decidedly not pregnant.

When I return from a bright but chilly walk, I decide to sign up for an online witchcraft class at Treadwell's Books with renowned witch Hannah Sanders. Treadwell's is one of the most famous occult and magic stores in the world and has a long repertoire of classes, both online and in-person at their London site. The class I have chosen is one about reading the omens of the natural world, of course. Yes, I've been an acolyte to symbolism for the majority of my life but a little more knowledge can never hurt. I knew that Hannah practised traditional witchcraft grounded in folklore, herbs and the old gods; this wouldn't be New Age mysticism – this was a class about the messages that animals and plants pass over the veil.

I shudder as I realise how much I am craving that ancient wisdom.

Hannah pops onto our screens and immediately I feel like I'm in safe hands. She sits at her kitchen table with steam cascading from a dark pot behind her and with herbs strung up in wizened bunches on either side. It's the kitchen of my wildest witchy dreams where a cauldron is always simmering to circulate warm energy throughout the house and the bitterness of mugwort collects at the back of your tongue. With a pull to my heart, I wish that I was on the other side of her dining room table with a strong cup of mint tea – I've been so cut off from my own witchy friends of late that I might as well be a lone red grouse. Hannah's horn-rimmed glasses, raven-dark hair and dark purple lips already tell me that this is someone who could be part of my inner circle but it is her deep, resonant voice that touches something below my ribs at my core and makes me stand to attention.

I am all ears.

Hannah starts by performing a meditation to ground us in the space. As my breath slows, I feel my eagerness turn slowly into a calm receptiveness. I am meant to be here – I am meant to have this knowledge. She tells us that cunning magic – the old folk magic that many still practise across the world – can help us to read the signs of the world and weave ourselves into it. Cunning folk are the wise women and folk healers of the land who many would have once gone to for healing charms, breaking spells of bad luck and divining the outcome of specific events. Practising cunning magic centres around knowing three things: the lore – customs, traditions and histories of the land; the gnosis – the meanings of the superstitions and synchronicities we observe around us; and the cunning knowledge and magic that we can use to affect certain events.

'It's our job as cunning people,' Hannah says, 'to be hyperattentive to the land and our observations. We offer magic as a service to others and knowing the signs of the land is our gift to them.'

I'm frantically scribbling down notes – tearing holes in the page with my spear-tipped Biro – as Hannah runs through the ways of feeling into the natural world to discern meaning. The weather, the land and the animals are all ways we can recognise the portents – the negative happenings – and the auspices –

the positive outcomes – coming our way. We only have to pay attention. By knowing intimately the mile and a half of land around your home through regular walks, you can build a picture of the area and notice the mutable signs that are passing through the land with messages. What are the constants and what are the signs flashing their flares? This is something I've done unconsciously in every place I've ever lived in: I've counted the magpies and checked for red skies in the morning, yes, but I've also noted on whose house the crows land, wondered why the dead nettle – a symbol of joy – has chosen to stay dormant in that particular spot this year, and have turned back as soon as the birdsong fell silent around me. I've done all these things intuitively, or perhaps from reading too many fantasy novels as a teenager, and never questioned it. But now I want to make a concerted effort to map the signs. Hannah even recommends keeping a log and drawing a chart of the local nature we spot in a wheel.

'But,' says Hannah, her voice stately and calm, 'it's the birds we have to pay closest attention to. Especially the black birds: not just the crows and the ravens; all black birds are linked with the knowledge of the underworld.'

My ears prick up. After all the black-feathered birds that have clouded my vision and taken up sentinel on my fence posts, I feel deftly attuned to their presence. But should I be worried about more of those black birds than I had first thought? Rooks – pure evil, yes. But blackbirds? Cormorants? This was something I'd have to look into further.

Hannah goes on. 'I have here a very specific kind of divination method. A frithir divination – coming from the Scottish word for "seer" – is a way that people can observe the birds to find the answer to a question. It's a form of augury, a type of bird divination that has been practised since the time of Ancient Rome, where an "augur" would study their movements and behaviour to determine the future. No major decisions were made in Rome without consulting an augur first.'

My pen is blazing.

Before advancing any military campaign, officials would have to get the '*aves admittunt!*' or 'the birds allow it!' sign from the augurs. We actually know a lot about the bird signs people looked for from the work of Cicero, who wrote about auspices in his *De Divinatione*. If you were facing to the south and birds flew in the east or the south, this was seen as a favourable sign. However, if birds were approaching you from the west or north, this was an unfavourable omen. The way you were facing made a huge difference. The same was true for bird calls, with it being unfavourable for a crow to call from the left but favourable if a raven called from the right.

'This frithir divination,' Hannah continues, 'is one you can perform yourself if you have a burning question you want to ask. To perform the charm, it is best to do so first thing in the morning. Speaking the words out loud, your answer to your question will appear to you as you open the door to your house.'

With those words, I know what I need to do. Auspices, here I come.

Witchcraft means a lot of different things to different people.

It can weave any number of disciplines into its silvery fabric: spellcraft, astrology and forms of divination, such as Tarot or reading the runes. For me, I have always been more interested in the herbalism side of things and have happily spent many hours with a wildflower guide in one hand and a bag of nettle, stitchwort and cleavers in the other, ready to trot home and make a tincture.

In my book *The Witch's Survival Guide: Spells for Healing from Stress and Burnout* I spent a lot of time trying to define what green witchcraft and Paganism actually are. There, I said that 'Pagan' is the overarching term for those with a spiritual connection with the land and the Four Elements. Many folk who follow Paganism believe nature to have a consciousness that can be tapped into through magical workings. We hold a reciprocal relationship with the 'more-than-human' world, honouring its cycles, leaving it offerings and giving thanks for its abundance. It is a very grounding path, one that celebrates Mother Earth; while a green witch is someone who celebrates the Earth's cycles and works with plants and herbs, but who also practises the art of spellcraft and ritual work.

Over the past few years, since witchcraft began its newest revival, I have had some feelings about the path witchcraft has taken that I've not been quite sure what to do with. Here goes:

Twenty-first-century witchcraft has become affiliated with sage sticks, crystals and good vibes.

But this is not the essence of true witchcraft.

New Age thinking has become so entwined with modern witchcraft that it feels almost impossible to separate out the two. This doesn't sit well with the earthen heart that wants to feel the dried, cracking mud on her skin and her hands clutching the pulse of living bark. I want to scream in the wild wood and feel its roots contract beneath my feet, rumbling the tightly packed animal bones that have lain in rest there over the centuries. I'm not averse to New Age thinking on its own – but I believe it can throw a blanket over the true cycles of life. Life also encompasses death, dying, sickness and trauma, but there are certain people in the New Age community who only focus on the light. If, goddess forbid, a terrible event occurs in your life, some would put a soft hand on your arm and paint on a pained expression to tell you it is your own fault when bad things come your way. None of the dark wisdom of the old Pagan ways is allowed in that space of live, laugh, spiritually bypass.

The latest iteration of witchcraft has a blatantly capitalist bent. New witches are told that they need a trunk full of sparkling goodies, rose quartzes and an apothecary-style cabinet of dried herbs to properly commit to their craft, plus an entirely new wardrobe of whimsy gothic Nicole-Kidman-à-la-*Practical-Magic* clothes to complete the aesthetic. Growing herbs is out, stockpiling them from Amazon is in. Yes, I would advise having a ritual outfit to wear during your practice but the idea that you have to 'look' like a witch to be a witch is concerning. This performative element is very strong and noticeable on social media. Full rituals – which were once seen as an incredibly personal and spiritual practice – are now filmed and put online even though it is surely difficult to commune with the divine with a ring light shining in the corner of the room? I've become quite weary of seeing beautiful young women in long dresses looking into the middle distance, sharing what appears to be a moment of spiritual solitude in nature. But the reality of those pictures is snap and move on. Next pose, check the camera, change the angle. How can I make this look more... 'witchy'? But where was the moment of spiritual connection? Did it happen at all? Or was it all just for the eyes of the internet? These photos are, of course, beautiful and elegant, but they are not what witchcraft and Paganism are.

These things are not a true reflection of this spiritual path: it is this version of witchcraft that told me it was my fault my baby was too sick to live.

This just isn't the witchcraft I signed up for. I signed up for something that does not shy away from the darkness. I signed up for full integration of the soul and the wild moments spent deep in nature; the reflection; the slap-dash nature of spells; the imperfections of the craft; the continual process of learning to understand the 'other-than-human' beings we share this planet with. Modern-day Pagans have one foot rooted in the structures and suburbs of twenty-first-century life and the other planted firmly between the rounded call of the tawny owl and the ridges of moss that line the furrows of the wildwood. We observe the cycles of life and find our place in its seasons, with nature as our deity – our provider and director. I am interested in the magic that is deeply grounded in the eternal magic of Mother Earth. I want the animal messengers of the old gods to whisper in my ear and tell me the news from beyond the veil. I want to be their mouthpiece.

But in spite of all my good intentions, that jagged plum pit of doubt was still firmly wedged in my head. What if it really had been my fault? What could I have possibly done in my life that was worth this level of pain? It must have been something truly awful. Yet I still racked my brains every day for any answer. Surely if I could figure it out, I could atone.

'Please give her back. Please give me another chance to prove that I could be a good mother.'

I hoped the divine was going to give me some answers.

The next morning I wake up and, still in my dressing gown, I stand in the hall facing towards the kitchen. Linnet sits on the carpeted stairs, soft little head poking through the railings. 'What are you doing *now*, Mother? Do I have to dial the loony bin with my tiny paws?'

I begin the frithir divination ritual that Hannah laid out the night before.

Phone in front of my face with the divination charm typed out on the screen, I start to say out loud:

'Gods over me, gods under me,

Gods behind me, gods before me:

I, on my path, you in my steps.'

I'm stumbling over my words as I walk slowly through my home, a clockwise loop of the downstairs – up the hall, into the kitchen, through to the dining room and living room, then back to the hall. I do this three times at a funereal pace.

'The augury made of Mother to son,

The offering made of Bride through her palm,

Saw you it, the well of wisdom at the source of light?

The augury made by the Mother for her children when light was dimmed?

Knowledge of truth that I shall truly see all of my quest.

Blessed spirits, Bride and Mother ever close,

Give me your eyes to see true and with grace they shall never fail.'

I put my hand on the front door handle and mutter the question I so desperately want the answer to under my breath. 'Will I get pregnant again this month?'

As instructed, I open the front door and put my hands on its sides, breath held.

Right in front of me, on the opposite neighbour's roof, are two wood pigeons. Copulating.

A grin breaks out on my face. 'Oh!' I say. A glimmer of positivity smacking me straight between the eyes. I know that wood pigeons are traditionally signs of peace, love and loyalty. Divination, I think I understand that message!

But the glimmer is hosed away with a clatter when a single magpie swoops up onto the roof from behind and knocks the amorous pigeons flying.

Oh.

My heart drops as if from a staggering height.

The magpie sits in the same spot the pigeons just left, cackling and holding its beak in the air triumphantly. I scowl and emit a low hiss from the back of my throat so that Linnet slinks to my side to see what's going on.

'Do you want me to get that bird, Mother?'

'Yes please, Linnet.'

Message received. It doesn't get much clearer than that.

You couldn't make this shit up and I want to slam the door in the world's face.

'You're spending a lot of time alone. Are you sure that's wise?'

Will had spoken to me with a furrowed brow the night before.

I clutch Sky Bunny close to my stomach. 'I see plenty of people.'

'But during the day – you're at home on your own. I'm not sure it's doing you any good.'

Whose fault is that? I wanted to snap. 'I'm fine,' I offer instead. But there are several reasons why I'm not making plans:

1. I'm so out of practice with making conversation that sometimes I just stare dumbly at my friends or answer in monosyllables before the quiver of tears at the back of my throat quavers. Who wants to be around a hot (less emphasis on the hot) grieving mess?

2. Being alone helps me to order my thoughts and steel myself against the fatigue, ready for my next trip into nature.

3. All I want to talk about is her.

I've got a lot of dead-baby thoughts to get in order. So I'm going out alone again and Will can't stop me.

Would he try and stop me?

Despite the blasts of early spring sunshine that filter through, the landscape is still contracted with cold. It bends the trees like walking canes, leeching life force away from the tips of their budded branches back down into the earth, where it is safe from frostbite. My shoulders are bunched around my ears as I follow the long, winding path down to a secret birding spot on the Wirral. It is a wild, off-the-map sort of place, fiercely guarded by locals; men in waterproof jackets and woolly hats are always at the ready to look as grumpy as possible to ward off any folk who might 'start getting ideas'.

It is a bleak landscape that I have become used to in my years of birding. Wading birds like sanderlings, dunlin and – my favourites – lapwings all gather at salty meres close to the coast up and down the country and here is no different. The tang of fish and brine, and the shriek of gulls always make me feel like a teenager again. Those days when I was just discovering the names of Britain's wild creatures and was filled with energy and coffee at five in the morning. You wouldn't catch me up and out before dawn these days but the early bird catches all the other birds, so they say.

Despite the knock of the magpie's message, I'm out again, my toes pulled by the threads of fine spring roots. The cold sunshine heightens my mood, even if I am still in my winter gloves, and there is a dogged compulsion in me to walk, walk, walk. Is it part of my continual quest for healing, armed with hiking boots and my binoculars? Or is it to get out of my living room, draped with memories of her? My house sometimes feels like a shrine to her. After Sky passed, people showered me with gifts: her birth chart in a little golden frame, a sky-blue eternal rose, a bracelet with her name on it. I display it all proudly in the living room but when people come to stay, I wrap her urn in a blanket and put it in the bottom of my wardrobe under the party dresses I haven't worn in years. That way, they won't have to feel their eyes flare when they look at the mantelpiece and quickly redirect their gaze to the TV. It is for their comfort but I feel guilty that my baby is hiding in the cupboard and not free to observe the living room with all its glittering Sky items.

The remembrances crush my heart daily.

But birds – birds will keep me light. Light and airy, so long as the magpies steer clear.

Across a mass of grassy tussocks, a spray of linnets (the birds, not the cat I've left at home pondering how to hack up a few corvids) are picking at last year's seed heads alongside the path and I stop to admire them, binoculars pressing my glasses into the bridge of my nose. The blushing red chests and crowns of their breeding plumage are bright against the buff and branch-coloured streaks on their backs. They are classic 'little brown jobs' but with an added touch of spice. They move like garden birds – quick eyes, sudden wing flitters – as they cling to long stems at forty-five-degree angles, prising out leftover autumn seeds like pearls from oysters.

I always wonder what the birds must think of us birdwatchers. We stand, right out there in the open, trying to slow our breathing and become as still as possible, holding black mechanical eyes up to our faces. We are fooling no one, of course. Pillars of hot whirring guts standing there for all to see; our white-roiling breath rising to gather above our heads out of our sight, but as clear as campfire smoke to those around us. Do the birds fear us? Ridicule us? Or perhaps pity us; unable as we are to cover our tracks and hide ourselves from the world as they do. The linnets twitter away, saying nasty things about my anorak.

Any naturalist or bird handler loves to tell you the infinitesimal size of a bird's brain – yes, an owl's eyes *are* indeed larger than its grey matter, a fact often said with a tone of loving mockery. But the immense capability of birds to migrate over large distances, communicate in the sky and, sometimes, even sleep on the wing is still a cluster of wonder to our 'superior' human brains.

I feel like a spindly tree with bulbous roots, my poorly chosen jeans cutting off the circulation at the knees, and I look down at my almost comically large walking boots protruding below – we are a family of big-footed women. You would have thought such a large base would be more likely to keep me steady and upright but, over the years, this has repeatedly proven not to be the case. I am not the most coordinated of people, which has led to me actually breaking my arm while birding. I have proceeded with slow, precise caution when going downhill ever since. This is something that has become ten times worse since giving birth – pregnancy felt like a constant state of acclimatising to a new centre of gravity. Now that my little anchor has gone, I am more Bambi-like than ever. I begin to pick my way through the mud downhill, enjoying the sucking squelch of my boots being pulled back down as I try to lift them and holding my arms out from my body for extra balance.

I follow the grassland down a secret slope into a wall of trees that has seen no one except the balding pates and camouflage hats of birdwatchers for the past few decades. The trees are stunted and twisted from the quirks of the marshland soil and, as I begin the descent down the wooden steps that lead through the wood, the wind tries to force me into my own hunched and peculiar state. In the summer, this copse would catch the quavering notes of redshank and the raucous racket of black-headed gulls floating over from the mere beyond. Right now, it is oddly silent.

Here, I feel starkly alone, away from the familiar rumblings of my home. It is too early in the day for hikers and too cold for any non-serious birdwatchers so, here by the marshes, I feel truly alone, my body light and filled with my own energy. It's been so long since I paused to feel my own essence that it actually feels unfamiliar. Uncanny.

There is a stillness in the air that reminds me of the moments of quiet before the red grouse spoke to me on the top of Pendle Hill. The quiet is pregnant and I await an explosion of birdsong that doesn't come. Silence is so rare these days. Has anyone on this side of the twenty-first century ever really heard it? This place feels suddenly rich with hidden meaning – it is a rift in time between pillars of sound; it feels like a portal.

I am surrounded by trees and the white light that comes through the bare branches seems to trigger something in me. It's like the world wobbles before my eyes. There is about to be a shift in my consciousness – I can feel it coming, the absence of noise making way for something with a denser mass; water forcing itself through a perforated hull.

Something magical is coming.

As I stand on the muddy path between the trees, I slip into an altered state of consciousness that I know well.

Here, colours sharpen, living things all have a more distinct outline and I can pinpoint sounds with stunning accuracy. It is a state that I believe has been used across time by our ancestors to keep them safe and to help them find food and water sources. There was even a recent case of missing children lost in the Amazon who were located by shamans using this trance-like state. Of course, I am no shaman but if I were to speak in this state, I feel like it would come out of my mouth in a very faraway voice, or maybe utter nonsense. This is a state that requires my inner voice only.

Did I *want* to shift my state here on my own in the woods so far from home? I hadn't consciously thought about it. I didn't start the process off in my mind, it just kind of... happened. When this occurs, I'd say that it *needed* to happen.

Why is this happening now? What am I supposed to be noticing? I wonder dimly.

Around me, I see the trees holding their branches high like guards with long swords; their criss-crossed arms alert and protective of me. In my trance state, I can feel their roots stretching out below me – deep, deep taproots anchoring this collection of birch, willow and alder metres deep into the earth. Sometimes they touch, like old friends checking in on each other's presence, and meld with the mycelial network and delicate nerve endings of the wood. I feel like my own feet have roots, keeping me standing still, upright, growing here. I send my consciousness down, down, into the earth, feeling the gentle wakefulness of early spring; the stillness of the roots, the layers of dead things, quiet and unfeeling. The earth is still awakening, not entirely out of its winter-induced slumber. I feel this sensation in my bones – I am half-awake too.

I know that I am witnessing nature's secrets below the earth's soft surface but why here? Why now?

A scuffling in the undergrowth shocks me so much that I am knocked back to my body with a gasp. My heart begins to race. What have I not sensed? What danger have I allowed myself to find?

Sky?

It is a male blackbird.

POOT POOT, it shrieks.

Another black death omen.

His yellow-ringed eye looks shrewdly out from the wet grasses, his delicate feet just about visible above the tricornered tracks in the mud. He cocks his head back slightly and looks like he is asking, 'What did you just see?' From my research after Hannah's class, I know blackbirds to be part of a mythic trio – the three noble birds of Rhiannon. Rhiannon, a Welsh mother goddess linked with the land and fertility, is connected with birds whose songs can transport listeners to a trance-like state or to the Otherworld itself. Could there be anything more beautiful than a male blackbird's song on long summer evenings?

I also know now that blackbirds in Celtic lore are thought to be the guardians of sacred gateways.

Maybe he is the guardian of the secrets I had just glimpsed under the ground. Or maybe something else – perhaps a path I am meant to follow. If I were performing an augury, would the blackbird dip his golden beak and tell me which route I needed to go down?

We continue our staring contest. He has his legs spread wide, ready to flee or ready to launch himself at me to protect his hidden knowledge.

We pass another minute frozen like this, locked in each other's thrall, until I check myself, nod respectfully and carry on along the path, pulling my feet out of the mud with a deep, tearing squelch. I am shaking a little, not looking back at the bird because I don't want him to know he has rattled me.

Even now, several months after Sky's death, the signs are still telling me that death clings to my aura.

I thought spring was supposed to come with new life.

In the bird hide, I spend an hour sweeping my binoculars back and forth over the mere and see the usual waders before heading back to the car. Flinging myself inside and cranking up the heat, I google 'blackbird symbolism' and read that blackbirds symbolise transformation and change, death and rebirth, while many cultures consider them to be guides between the living and the dead.

Transformation and change.

I tap my fingers on the steering wheel.

Well, that's not all doom and gloom really, is it? Much like the Death Tarot card, transformation is all about endings but also about rebirth. There is always light in the darkness; not that I have seen much of it of late. I think back to that feeling of shifting between worlds and start to believe with all my might that I was supposed to meet that blackbird today – perhaps he was an emissary from the goddess herself.

I am done with crows. I am done with curlews and magpies. Perhaps my involuntary altered state of consciousness was showing me that I'm moving into a new era of my life.

Now wouldn't that be something?

I open the car window a crack and say, 'Thank you, Mr Blackbird!' into the empty car park.

Chapter Eight

Hare

She was long – which was absolutely a surprise to no one – like her tall, thin, gangly parents.

She had long, ethereal fingers. I'd always been told I had a pianist's fingers but now every time I looked down at my hands, I saw her hands.

And she was absolutely beautiful.

Sky was so incredibly wanted. We tried for her for so long that I had almost given up hope.

In the seventeen months it took us to get pregnant with Sky, everyone else was pregnant. Everyone. Just not me. I would listen to their stories – friends, colleagues, acquaintances. They'd try once. Pregnant. Smoke and drink heavily for fifteen years. Pregnant. Think of the unhealthiest person you can. Pregnant and thriving. People get pregnant by accident – abort the baby or keep it. A 'friend' tells me on my thirty-fourth birthday she just got a positive pregnancy test and ruins the day. My sister gets pregnant the month after we start trying and I have to hide the hard-edged coil of envy that threads through my guts. Another friend's sister has a cryptic pregnancy and doesn't know she's going to have to give birth until she is eight centimetres dilated in A&E.

Why not me?

Why not me?

Before getting pregnant, I had asked my Tarot cards and received Temperance again and again – the fourteenth card in the deck. Moderation. Balance. 'Be patient, it will come. Be patient.' But I had no patience coating my bones in white, velveted calm. I had only desperation – a deep fear of being left behind without a family to call my own.

How can we want something so much, something that we've been told 'will happen, don't worry, just relax' and for it to be *this* hard?

But the hardest part had been yet to come for me.

It isn't until tragedy strikes that you notice the prams. This is why, during the Second World War, mothers or women with prams were often used as spies for one side or the other. Who notices the mothers with their innocuous smell of baby wipes and fruit snacks? Mothers fly under the radar except to other mothers or those who are desperately trying to become one of them. After Sky's death, there seemed to be a legion of them. They are clustered together in cafes. They are ready to accelerate around every suburb corner. How can so many people be having babies? I thought we were in the midst of a bloody fertility crisis? Or the 4B movement? Or so the internet graphs and online articles tell me.

I change my walking routes to avoid the nearby lake and the playgrounds I've never noticed before. Before I leave the house, I take a second glance at my phone to check the time. School drop-off slots are a no-go. I go to the city more often than I would like because the chance of seeing a baby lessens. The busy streets are filled with hooded teenagers with slicked-back hair clutching Stanley cups, businessmen with a spare tyre or two, and fresh-faced Gen Z interns not yet beaten down by the world. A reprieve. But in the countryside, I'm jealous of even the ewes in the fields, suckling their lambs after a single tupping last winter. It doesn't get much more desperate than that.

But still, there are babies on my Instagram feed. Pregnancy announcements that feel like a high kick to the gut. An ex-colleague posts a picture of his newborn, which has the same name we had originally picked out for Sky: I spend the next two days in bed. Those joyfully posted ultrasound pictures are my absolute nightmare. I do not want to see it. I am part of the empty-armed ranks who do not want to know.

In that moment, I am not happy for you. I hate you. And I can't help it. I don't want to hate you but why do you have a healthy baby and not me?

'And now we have to start all over again,' I sob to Vicky, the wonderful bereavement midwife who has called me every single week without fail. Always calm, always cheerful, always willing to talk about silly telly and cats. Will and I may be trying for another baby but my physical body is still in ruins – not from the birth but because I've forgotten how to look after myself. Just as the house is in an utter state, so am I. The person who remains is stiff, small and slumped over like she is trapped in the curve of a conch shell.

On hearing my noisy sniffles on the phone to Vicky, Linnet hurtles up the stairs from her living room cushion and prrrps her way onto the bed with a single bound. She is purring so loudly as she presses her two front paws hard into my thigh.

'Don't panic, Mother! All is well – I have arrived. Stop your water loss.'

Of course, I start laughing.

'Thank you, Linnet!' I giggle and Vicky laughs too as I start to feel my dark cloud lighten.

'Awww, they always know what to do, don't they?' she says.

Yes, they always, always do.

I am heading to Scotland alone for many reasons: the wildlife, the sea air and to completely defragment my brain.

Goddess, I need this.

I have recently let my working hours creep back up to full-time, recording my hours on a Google Sheet and making copious cups of tea to make sure I am some semblance of awake for my Monday morning 8.15 meeting. But this time, I am not about to work myself into the ground. Not like before. I can't do that again – not for the sake of my health or for my fertility. It is time to start taking my own advice and work normal hours like a sane person.

And besides, there are a whole host of other reasons:

1) Will hasn't processed his grief at all and, instead, spends as much time out of the house as possible. The bereavement midwife team tells me that men deal with their grief much later, often pushing it down into their chest cavities while they throw themselves into work. I am 'Grieving Mother Without a Child', he is 'Man Who Works'. I resent Will for doing this, for going back to the office and leaving me curving over my empty belly in bed. I know it is an ugly feeling but why should he – the only person who had been through this with me step by step, blow by blow, in the hospital – have a reprieve from this daily hell?

From the loss of her? I wanted to grip him by his shoulders and force him to look at the ragged pieces of bone and mottled complexion I'd become. *This*, I wanted to say. *This is how you should be.*

2) Being out of the house away from Sky's urn would surely be helpful to me.

3) Out in true nature, there are a whole lot more positive signs to spot than in my magpie-riddled garden.

Spurred on by the blackbird, I was on high alert for the signs.

I've settled on the Lowlands, west of Dumfries – an area I've never been to before – and have vague ideas of what wildlife might be around but, to be honest, I'll be happy to just face-plant some leaves and I get the feeling I'll cry the first time I see a wading bird. I need to touch a tree like my life depends on it.

Maybe now is the time to take stock of my healing journey and see how far I've come. I fear I am not as far down the road as I had hoped to be. On this trip, I will be the furthest away from her that I have ever been – far from her palmful of ash on the mantelpiece, with its too-large urn, and far from the places I had been with her. It is a sobering thought and one brought into stark contrast by the wide open skies that hit me as I drive north.

It's nearly Beltane now – the Pagan festival of fertility and the fairy realms. Spring has taken its time to arrive, leaving everyone in a fuggy state of dis-ease; still slurping soup and plodding around in their winter socks while the late frosts and rain have killed off the first buds. But now as I'm driving via a winding path of out-of-the-way nature reserves, the world has recovered and everything is yellow against the thick blue backdrop of sky. The lanes are bordered by thick cloaks of dandelion and lesser celandine – Scotland has dusted off its welcome mat to find itself a bright, pulsing gold below.

I am amazed that, despite everything, sunshine *does* actually make most things feel better.

Gorse is all around and I drive with the windows down to catch nosefuls of its coconutty scent. Of course, I shouldn't have been surprised at the sight of it all, as a phrase commonly associated with long-flowering gorse is, 'When gorse is out of bloom, kissing is out of season!' You could spot those lurid yellow flowers a mile away. These thorny shrubs weather the high winds of the coast, allowing the coastal breeze to spread their seaside scent and attract more pollinators. In Ancient Ireland, gorse branches were thrown onto the Beltane ritual bonfires to bring love, fertility and protection to the community, with the flowers often used in bridal bouquets – a beautiful way to bring colour and life in the colder months when flowers were scarce.

I think about the magical properties of the colour – that rich egg-yolk yellow. It stands for clarity, joy, confidence, knowledge, inspiration – and feel my cheeks smiling. I feel so honoured to be here amongst these Beltane flowers just before such a potent fertility festival. What I wouldn't give to be a bare-shouldered Beltane maiden with yellow gauze wound through my hair like the ribbons of a maypole. This is exactly what I've needed. My smile intensifies as I turn into the drive of where I'm staying, only moments after passing a sign reading 'Kirkcudbright: Artists' Town'.

The Airbnb I've booked into has a distinct theme. Cows. Of the Highland variety to be exact. Cushions, bedding, kitchen trays, kitschy cups, keyring – all decorated with hairy, orange cows. I'm not going to lie, I like it.

After a day of driving, my legs might be two bits of string sewn into my hips and I want nothing more than to flop down on my cow bed but instead I vow to return their blood supply by getting out and exploring the local area.

Kirkcudbright (pronounced ker-Coo-bree for those of us not well-versed in Scottish diction) is a charming pastel-painted town along the River Dee. A row of bookshops, boutiques, galleries and salons is all closed but glints like an animé village. The bright, low-slung light along the estuary scalds my eyes and I squint out at egrets and redshank ankle-deep in the silty strait. Is that a tear in my eye? I can't quite be sure.

I follow the steep streets through a caravan park and a football pitch to where the woods begin.

It hasn't been five minutes when a flash of colour catches my eye and my head spins so fast that the trees stutter in and out of focus.

A red squirrel.

There the wee laddie is. Welcome to Scotland!

Hunched on a silver-birch branch, he is watching me with eyes as sharp as a kestrel's. As far as I am aware, no convicted or suspected witches ever had the cheery red squirrel as their animal familiar, but under this one's gaze, I could almost believe he was the guardian of a witch's cottage or the mossy entrance to the Otherworld.

I have entered the wilderness and my spirit sighs with relief.

The next day, I wake up to the sound of rabbits nibbling the short grass outside my window and a troop of Highland cows mooing brazenly. The sunlight through their fuzzy mops makes halos around each cow.

I drink my cow-cup of tea, then I'm off.

I have planned a full-day walk around the point of Ross a few miles down the road. The day is so bright after weeks of Lancashire grey rolling in from the moors; this landscape of infinitely blue skies and sea couldn't be more different. I test out tying my waterproof around my waist, feeling the late-April sun palm my arms and am half-restored already, like I'm a pale plant that's been kept in a cupboard too long. The sea sparkles, and the winking gems of waves make me hold my breath in excitement.

Along the lurid green clifftops close to Kirkcudbright, I am struck by the silence. The yellow gorse thickets around me often obscure the blue of the sea and, with it, the sound and the motion of the wind. For what seems like infinite stretches of time, all I can hear is my own breathing, like I am a mirage that only I can see amongst the golden flowers. In this thorny realm, where my pulse is the only pulse to have ever existed, I start to feel the thinness of the veil in this place: Beltane is coming.

Beltane has to be my favourite festival of the year.

Traditionally on Beltane – which falls between 30th April and 1st May each year – communities would gather together around a large bonfire, allowing the fire to protect and cleanse them, ridding them of any negativity from the previous season. However – just as with Halloween, the festival's direct counterpoint of the year – it is also the time when the veil between our world and the mystical Otherworld is said to be at its thinnest. In her book *Thin Places*, Kerri ní Dochartaigh says: 'Heaven and earth, the Celtic saying goes, are only three feet apart, but in thin places that distance is even shorter. They are places that make us feel something larger than ourselves, as though we are held in a place between worlds, beyond experience.'[16]

ní Dochartaigh speaks of the wild places in nature, the liminal spots; they are places that provide us with glimpses of another spiritual plane melding with our own. She talks about their shapeshifting transparency; things with invisible particles, just like sea mist.

Beltane is a time when these 'thin places' emerge into gossamer-like being. It is a time to catch a shimmering glance of Fairyland hanging between two hawthorn trees. A time to hear the whisper of a fairy messenger – a rabbit, a hare or maybe a fox – sent out to lure you back to their realm. Ancient Celts believed that rabbits burrowed underground to flit into the spirit world and carry messages from the living to the dead and from humankind to the Fae. Beltane isn't all giggling maidens and cherry blossom.

Viewed under this lens, Beltane is just as much a festival to celebrate and honour the dead as Samhain, but perhaps the longer daylight hours and the shimmering blossom are symbols of hope that we can sometimes struggle to find at the flip side of the year. The twisted trees, the scent of green life in the air and the coming together as a community around the twilit fires remind us of the fragility of time – how life and death are always so closely bound together.

As I walk the cliffs above this liminal, thin place where the Irish Sea meets the Atlantic, I decide to honour the life that resides in Beltane and pluck a gorse flower from the coarse bush beside me. I bring it to my lips and let it fall on my tongue. It tastes like spring sunshine.

I close my eyes, feeling into the silence of the gorse thicket. I am out of space, out of time. Just me, the silent flowers and the blazing blue up above.

'Bring me my baby,' I whisper and feel the sound sink into the space, vacuumed up through some trapdoor to the Otherworld. My mouth feels empty and papery afterwards. I breathe out and forge on with achy legs.

A couple of miles later, the gorse thins and I am trudging across farm fields; the cow-trodden mud has stiffened to high peaks in the sun and each step threatens to roll my ankle. Just as my walk has reached its most precarious point, a dark flash streaks across my vision on the hillside up ahead. What is that? A goat?

When I realise it is a hare, I'm flabbergasted.

Hares are massive here.

I yank up my binoculars and watch the huge creature nibbling at the grass, completely incongruous with its surroundings.

Someone who has never seen a hare before (or who has never watched *Donnie Darko* late at night) might take a step back from this deformed bunny rabbit. Indeed, the hare has a slightly baffling appearance. Bulging eyes, ears like antlers and a scruffy, haunted appearance as if it has just been dragged backwards out of hell. It holds itself so stiffly and awkwardly like an automaton programmed to strike at any second.

But I hold its strange form firmly in the range of my binoculars, knowing its symbology only too well.

The brown hare (*Lepus europaeus*), believed to have been introduced to the UK during Roman times or even earlier, is now considered a naturalised species, one that caught at our imagination a very long time ago.

This long-limbed loper mainly lives in open farmland, scrub and hedgerows, feeding on vegetation and the bark of young trees and shrubs, but, quite surprisingly, you won't find a brown hare in a burrow – contrary to popular belief – instead finding refuge in shallow ground depressions or grassy forms called scrapes. When startled, they can be seen bounding across fields, using their powerful hind legs to propel themselves forward in a zigzag path to throw you off their scent.

It seems that almost every culture across the world has mythology associated with the hare. Many of these myths are related to fertility, abundance and renewal, most likely due to the hare's rapid reproduction rates and prolific numbers around Beltane, when the world is just starting to grow again. Indeed, fertility goddesses such as Germanic Eostre and Norse Freyja are often shown with a hare by their side, ready to spring into action and incite fertility amongst the locals. One Celtic custom was to place a rabbit or hare skin under the bed to increase fertility and fulfilment – which, just as with the fox tail tradition, wasn't so fulfilling for the hare. This image of the hare makes sense, hopping merrily along with its small, ruffled leverets as they celebrate the bounty of spring. But another large part of the hare's mythology is its association with rebirth and transformation, perhaps because of its deep connection with the moon and lunar energies.

The symbol of the moon-gazing hare has been seen across cultures in Japan, China, Mexico and Europe for millennia

– the hare looking up with its ears slicked along its back, the full moon rising above it, its eyes filled with otherworldly knowledge – so much so that historians are often confused at how this symbol could possibly have infiltrated so far. In Chinese folklore, the most famous hare is the Moon Rabbit (commonly accepted as a hare), often referred to as the Jade Rabbit. This legend tells the story of a hare that lives on the moon, where it is believed to be pounding herbs to create an elixir of immortality. The Moon Rabbit is often depicted as a companion to the moon goddess Chang'e, who is said to have consumed the elixir, which resulted in her ascending to the moon. Hares, despite my daytime sighting, are primarily crepuscular and nocturnal, darting through the trees under the light of the waxing moon. While the ancient symbol of the moon-gazing hare may once have held other meanings, nowadays it has become a well-used symbol of mysticism and the connection between the earthly and the celestial.

A symbol of the liminal, as it were.

Is it purely their nocturnal nature that has given hares their reputation of darting between other worlds? Or is it their relationship with the witching world?

In Nordic countries, the hare has a close association with witchcraft. An article in *Folklore* describes how:

> [w]itches are supposed to be able to create a supernatural creature which is given life and sent out in order to steal milk or dairy produce; in southwest Sweden, and once or twice in Norway, this creature is said to resemble a hare, although mostly looking somewhat different from a natural hare. The most common name for the animal

is mjölkhare, 'milkhare' ... A milkhare is usually said to be made from heddles and bits of wood or, in parts of the area, from bits of besoms and scrubbing brooms. The making of the creature may be accompanied by the witch selling herself to the Devil and a satanic pact. In northern Sweden and Finland the milk-thief is often given blood from the owner to bring it to life, or a communion wafer is used.[17]

In 1662, Isobel Gowdie from Auldearn in the Highlands of Scotland claimed to have entered into a pact with the Devil and attended coven meets. She provided vivid descriptions of these gatherings, including their rituals, spells and the spirits they conjured and spoke to. She also revealed that she possessed the ability to turn into a hare to carry out the Devil's deeds. To do this, she would chant:

I shall go into a hare,
With sorrow and sych and meickle care;
And I shall go in the Devil's name,
Ay while I come home again.

To return to her human form, she would say:

Hare, hare, God send thee care.
I am in a hare's likeness now,
But I shall be in a woman's likeness even now.[18]

This link between hares, witches and Paganism seems to have a connection with the rise of Christianity and the demonisation of hares. In Celtic culture, the hare was revered and would never be eaten or killed except for on Beltane. As time went on and the Christians worked their own forms of magic (or indoctrination), the hare's association with ideas of rebirth and renewal were replaced by Jesus's resurrection story – handily falling at exactly the same time of year.

Hares are mainly solitary creatures. Unlike their more sociable second cousins, the humble rabbit, they can be spotted as a lone pair of dark ears poking out over the corn stalks. Much as the witch herself has been ostracised from society, stirring her cauldron in her house on the edge of the village, the hare is often seen alone and looking like an unusual visitor to the land. Rabbits, huddled together with their cute, rounded faces, ping-pong ball bodies and liquid eyes, couldn't look more different. The hare's bony, sinewy body, its topaz-coloured eyes and its haggard hunch are enough to make anyone think of something carrying an unpleasant message from the Underworld. When you see them side by side, it's not hard to see why the hare is called the unlucky one.

But a discussion of hares wouldn't be complete without a mention of the 'mad' March hare. Brown hares are most often seen out and about during early spring, when the breeding season is at its peak. During this time, the bucks become more active and aggressive in their pursuit of females or does, chasing, boxing and running about erratically, almost like the mental cheese has slid off their cracker. Although we might commonly associate this behaviour with male hares, the buck's boxing partner is most likely to be a female warding off unwanted amorous advances.

It's quite a sight to behold and might have been the final nail in the coffin for the hare's reputation.

Why isn't any animal associated with fertility ever a straightforward sign?

The hare on the hill stops. Turns its head and fixes its buggy, amber eyes on me. It watches where I stand for half a second and then darts – flees – a flurry of strong, long limbs forcing the ground away as it zigzags off. Surely this mystical creature, one hundred metres away, doesn't think I'm about to use my puny leg muscles to fire up a cross-country chase? With my binoculars, I track its erratic path into a gorse bush. Safe. Cocooned in spikes.

I take myself onto the road, finally away from the jagged mud track, and walk to the headland to where the hare lies in hiding. From there, after a quick cheese sandwich, I can begin the journey back to my Highland cow haven. But I'm not halfway up the hill when the hare is right in front of me again.

I freeze.

This is not the time of day for seeing hares; but, in fact, this is the first and only time I've seen one out in broad daylight with the sun behind it. Gangly and struck with the glassy knowing of a terrible secret, its haunted eyes permeate my soul; amber burning into my retinas as we are locked in this mutual stare. What kind of sign is this? Does the night hold too many dangers for this hare? Are food sources scarce under the light of the moon? Or is it trying to get my attention?

What Beltane faery message am I about to intercept?

As if in response to a whip crack, the creature darts back and forth in an irregular line, leading me forward. I feel like I'm tied to an invisible string; the hare snagging it on gorse thorns posts to keep me attached and following with ragged breath. It doesn't leap away into the bushes that had hidden it before but keeps urging me forward, rising up the hill. I half expect to hear its claws gripping into the earth as the sound of the sea has fallen away again. I am suspended in ghostly 'thin' air, streaming from the wake of the hare.

Where is it luring me?

At this moment, held in the grip of the signs, I'm excited to find out where. I imagine the hare pointing its nose to a swaddle of leverets in their wide open scrape yet completely invisible to the naked eye. The hare would turn back and look at me with that half-mad glint in its eye and say, 'All this will be yours soon.'

It finally darts to my right onto a ledge of rock at the base of a clump of gorse. It turns its haunted expression to me. Wild-eyed. Manic.

'What are you trying to tell me?' I call.

It only twitches its nose and finds the safety of a gorse bush once again. I see its white bobbin tail for only a fraction of a second more before it is thoroughly consumed by the thorns, absorbed into the thinness of the world.

I stand for a few moments, unsure of what to do now. Wait? Re-find my route? The second option seems pretty boring now but, bar shaking the hare out from behind the wall of yellow, there is little more I can do.

As I continue my walk, the sea crashes into my eardrums again, bringing me back to the headland of Ross and away from the Fairy Queen. It makes me feel slightly dizzy, as if I have just reached a new altitude, tearing back into the fabric of reality. I shake myself and continue my trudge across mud-slick spring fields, dodging cows with spindly newborn calves, wishing I hadn't worn a red rucksack. I disturb several more hares over the course of the next hour (or is it the same one, determined to deliver its otherworldly message?) and smile every time. But as the day goes on, I realise that, thanks to the bitterly cold winter we've just had, perhaps these are the 'mad' March hares, slightly late to the game in their breeding season, erratically trying to catch the scent of a female in oestrus over the coconut scent of gorse during the daylight hours.

I huff. I guess I'm not the chosen one after all. No secret message, just the flux of seasonal shifts and animals acting accordingly.

But I can keep hoping.

It makes me wonder, though: have I been spotting symbols on my quest for healing or just the signs of the season? It is a question that breeds more questions than answers because if the world isn't trying to show me my path through its many signs and symbols, then...

What is there to believe in at all?

That evening, I return to the Airbnb and empty a handful of fresh gorse flowers into a mug. My hand smells sweet and faintly tropical from cradling them there for so long, the scent stitched into the lines and snags on my palm. In the mug of steaming water, the scent deepens to something more bitter and green as the petals stew. I strain the drink and bring it over to the bed.

It isn't quite Beltane but I am in a fertile sort of mood.

I sit on the edge, looking out at the Highland cattle who have migrated to the other side of the field to catch the late sunset colours in their shaggy manes. I visualise a string of spring light beaming down from the sky and through the crown of my head, threading through my body like green, mossy spider's silk, and out of my base into the ground. I feel anchored in place – bolt upright on the patchwork quilt, breathing consciously and connected to the sky and earth.

I lift the mug to my face and blow, cascading steam over the room. The gorse tea feels vital and pulsing with heat, its coconut scent braiding my hair and coating my scalp. I whisper into the mug:

'I am fertile. My body is strong. I am ready to receive a healthy baby.'

I prepare myself to take a sip. 'I am ready.'

Chapter Nine

Ladybird

May 2024

'The Sky Garden looks beautiful! Come and see.'

Earlier in the year, I'd gone into a frenzy of seed collecting and had been storing them in the cupboard above the cooker since January, keeping them warm until spring. My plan was to create a small garden that would bloom blue in colour – blue for my Sky. Her soul would always be the same twenty-one grams but I could grow things in her honour that would become bigger, wirier and taller than she had ever been. I bought some heavy terracotta and blue pots and clustered them together in the patio's sunniest spot, imagining how it would look once the sea of blue petals had amassed above them. I had this vision of gazing out my kitchen window to a haze of buzzing blue, covered in butterflies and pollinators. There would be forget-me-nots, sweetpeas, cornflowers – the lot; anything I could find to get things bluer in here. In the same spirit, I'd written messages to Sky on two bright blue ribbons and tied them to our cherry tree back in winter. In the Pagan tradition, these are called clooties – coming from the Scottish word 'cloot' meaning 'cloth'. Clooties are strips of cloth or ribbons tied to trees, often near sacred wells or springs as part of a ritual offering or a request for healing from the gods. Something about seeing those bright pieces of ribbon made me nod with the knowing that I had done the right thing.

In the colder months, the clooties had sparkled with ice droplets, shining out as the brightest things in the garden amongst the bare, winter-saturated branches. Then in early spring, I had loved to see them entwined with the white cherry blossom. I looked forward to seeing them in every season and finding out how the north weathered them.

In March, I'd woken up one morning and decided that today was the day to crunch my fingers into the newly thawed earth and sort out the seed trays. The first flower to emerge was a morning glory – purple with white stripes – not blue but close enough (do you know how hard it is to find more than five blue flowers?).

And now, my little blue garden – the Sky Garden – is starting to properly bloom.

It has taken its time to get going, despite the seeds being planted in the first days of spring. I suppose we all sometimes need extra time to decide what our futures are going to look like. There were a few failed germinations – I'm a herb not a garden flower grower – so quite a lot of my plants never made it to the pots (the irony isn't lost on me). But the thing about the sky is that it holds a thousand colours.

And so I planted a sunrise: red campion, borage, lavender, geraniums, begonias, a single sunflower and a yellow tea rose given to me by my family called 'Sunny Sky'. The garden itself, new as it was, started to show the shades of the sky at different times of the day – from the soft pre-dawn lilacs, the hazy pinks of early morning and the blasts of midday sunshine.

Some days, when the sun was at its peak, the orange-tip and brimstone butterflies appeared with their uneven threads of flight. In the dead of night, I can only imagine that the moths appeared – at least, I hope they did. The bees hadn't quite discovered the garden yet but I knew they would come in time, when summer kicked off next month. I couldn't wait to bring my yoga mat out here and sun myself surrounded by the soft hum of hoverflies, beetles and bees; life's favourite music.

'What do you think?' I ask Will nervously as he stuck his head out of the conservatory. He is the real gardener around here, after all.

'It looks wonderful, babe,' he says, a solemn set to his mouth. 'You've done a really good job.' I don't know if he's thinking about Sky or about the obsessive glint I've had in my eye over the past few months whenever I've mentioned the garden. My determination has paid off though.

He puts an arm around my shoulder as we both look down at the blooming pots, the blue clooties tied to the cherry tree rippling in the spring breeze. I close my eyes, feeling the heat of his ever-warm body against me, catching the familiar scent of the shower gel we share that makes us smell like twins. This has been a hard journey for us both to shoulder and one that could leave many couples in tatters with the sheer force of will it takes to cut oneself through the day-to-day slog. I hope he is back to keeping me upright instead of leaving me sprawled and rudderless. When I open my eyes, his eyes are blue as forget-me-nots on mine.

I didn't know until months later – when I was trying to find more blue flowers for next year's Sky Garden – that the term 'blue flower' had many different meanings.

The 'blue flower' is a central symbol of early nineteenth-century Romanticism – the era of Keats, Byron and awe of the natural world. The term first appeared in the 1802 novel *Heinrich von Ofterdingen*, by the German writer Novalis. In the story, the hero dreams of a blue flower that evokes a deep sense of yearning and spiritual connection in him. For the Romantics, the blue flower was often used as a metaphor for transcendence and the unattainable.

I knew that planting my little blue cornflowers wouldn't bring her back but I hoped that if she looked down from above the cherry tree, she would see the ribbons in her own colour and watch as the flowers stretched up towards her – the loving hands of a mother who could no longer hold her.

There comes a time in mid-May when I start to notice a shift.

It begins with a remembering of how to notice the world. I register the tinkling of birdsong at five a.m., the way the dawn skips quickly into sunshine and the way the flurries of warm rain riffle the leaves of the apple tree. I notice the white bursts of blossom that have emerged at sporadic intervals down the hawthorn branches. I press my face to them, narrowly avoiding the spines that are supposed to ward off sparrows and foxes, hoping to catch the scent of sweet decay they exude. I smell the first wafts of it and feel something mend inside my head. A torn seam sutures itself, propelled by the needle of spring.

I begin to have creative ideas again that I jot dot in my blue leatherbound diary; I drink my silly hot-girl green juice that I was influenced to buy from TikTok, and it genuinely makes me feel better; I go to the gym twice a week and am making a serious dent in my strangely angled mum tum. Towards the end of the month, I sit down and count the days: it has been over three weeks since I cried.

I am repairing. The grey pre-dawn fuzz of grief is beginning to lift.

There is no denying that the holiday has done me a lot of good so that, against all odds, I feel like I could sit down at the dining room table and write and write and write. Or at least look studious and maybe even slightly whimsical without an hourly tear break. I feel like a second eyelid has just opened up under the creased and battered pair that I've been wearing all winter, and I am able to see the world in a brighter spectrum of colour than before. I plunge down the country lanes that I have walked hundreds of times but have never seen in such splendour before; the dog rose hedgerows are starting to sprout jaggedy tufts of leaves along thorn-speckled stems and the spry fingers of sticky cleavers look almost too vibrantly green for this world.

As I walk, a magpie skids out of the hedge and onto the road ahead of me. I slow, wary of this demon bird with its funeral-lily feathers, ready to chase it out of my onward path. But as quickly as it appears, so does another.

Relief floods through me like spilled golden honey.

I can't quite believe it but as I continue my daily walking loop I see more pairs of magpies. There! And there – all flying in front of me no more than twenty feet away. Perhaps it is the same pair, flashing their black eyes at me, saying, 'Here we are, another two for you to add to the count!'

One for sorrow, two for joy, again and again at regular intervals.

Yes, it is spring and the birds are naturally pairing up. But this flamboyant display of black-and-white feathers feels like a message that I am so very willing to hear. This is the year's most fertile time. Perhaps it will be mine too.

As the days go on, my eyes are flared open to look for the signs – if only a stork would fly over the house and make the whole guessing game a lot easier. I begin to see robins everywhere, establishing their new springtime territories alongside me as I propel myself forward through the lanes. Their symbolism flashes up in my head – rebirth, new beginnings, joy. There is a flurry of life happening around me. The omens are disintegrating and being replaced by symbols of brighter times ahead. Surely this is a miracle. One morning, I look out the bathroom window and see something white in the garden that has fallen directly below Sky's two blue clooties on the cherry tree. Morbidly, I think it is a spray of pigeon feathers left over from the local sparrowhawk so I go to investigate and find a willow branch stuck directly into the ground, its white catkins making it look like a hand wearing many silver rings. I puzzle at this for some time, looking up at the blue ribbons then down at the willow branch. What does this mean? Surely it means something important. Google tells me that the willow tree symbolises our capability to withstand hardships, loss and difficult emotions. They are survivors and scrappy, shallow-rooted symbols of rebirth.

The auspicious placement of the branch trickles over me and I pick it up to plant it in a pot near to the house, as close to my daily life as it can be.

But while all this tear-free time is liberating, I feel more than an ounce of guilt to be doing something other than deep grieving. The Wheel of the Year is turning quicker than normal – was everyone aware of this? – and I am caught up in its green flow through the blossom-filled portion of the year. The magnolia, apple and cherry trees in my garden proudly display every ounce of energy they've been saving up over the winter months through their white halos and I feel like I'm coming out of this. Maybe. More lined and grey-haired than before, yes. Wiser, definitely. But it seems I have crossed a line, a line drawn under the worst of this experience. I squeeze my eyes shut and hope to the goddess that it is the finish line. With that thought, I nudge the tip of the needle into my stomach and push the plunger.

Our IVF journey so far hasn't been a straightforward one. In all honesty, I don't see how it ever could be. They say that IVF can be an emotional rollercoaster and – boy – they weren't wrong. The constant assault of alien hormones, the last-minute scans, the self-administered injections and the anxious checking of the upward curve of my stimulated eggs on the little graph has left me an absolute nervous wreck. I'd known next to nothing about IVF when we first started the process, so the twice-daily hormone injections had been quite the surprise. But it had been the uncertainty of it all that had caused the most panic: one missed injection could make all the difference between a baby and starting all over again.

For anyone undergoing IVF, I would say this: go into it with nerves of steel. It is not as easy as them popping a fertilised egg inside you. Although I wish it were.

An average round of IVF looks like this:

A clinician will check your ovarian reserve and if things look good (yay!), you can then proceed with treatment to stimulate as many of your follicles (each containing an unripe egg) as possible. Treatment involves two self-administered daily injections for two weeks – which will leave your abdomen looking like a junkie's. My belly button seems lost in the sea of red and purple track marks that I hide under soft clothing so as not to draw any more blood than is absolutely necessary. I trail my thumb over the faded red scars from the amniocentesis and where the doctor had administered Sky's potassium shot. Will they be there forever? Will I have to see those marks of remembrance every time I look down?

While you are undertaking the injection portion of your treatment, you will also go for scans every two days where the consultant checks the size of your follicles and how many eggs it might be possible to harvest. After two intensive weeks of syringes, I have to take a very specific 'trigger injection' twelve hours before my egg retrieval, which will send as many eggs as possible into maturity.

Truly, what an incredible time to be alive, when all of *this* wonder is possible.

On the day of the trigger injection, I am the most hormonal I have ever been in my life. I am stuttering and anxious five minutes before the allotted time that I have to take the shot as I grapple with the syringe that I have to make up myself. In my worked-up state, I break the glass twisty-bottle of saline solution, cut my fingers and start bleeding profusely all over the dining table.

'SHIT, SHIT, SHIT, SHIT,' I scream, alone in the house with no one to help me.

With two minutes to go before I have to have the injection, I ring our clinician, sobbing, and she calmly walks me through the steps with another bottle of solution as I continue to bleed steadily onto the floor.

The trigger injection stings and I wince as I pull out the needle with shaky hands.

The decision to go down this path hadn't been easy but I am all in. We had recently been for fertility tests at the hospital and I was found to have polycystic ovaries while Will had an issue with his sperm. He had three times the normal amount but... only one per cent of them were the right shape.

Which put a spanner in the works.

We had been told it is likely that the only way I would get pregnant was through IVF, or rather ICSI – an Intracytoplasmic Sperm Injection – where – unlike typical IVF where the sperm and egg are left in a petri dish to self-fertilise – a sperm is manually injected into the egg by an embryologist. The NHS consultant had given us zero ways to improve our chances naturally and had put us on a waiting list for ICSI, which had promptly been lost in the system. Our new wait time was eighteen months, and so here we were at a private clinic, all signed up to our payment plan.

But we had got pregnant once before, hadn't we?

Maybe we could get pregnant again naturally.

Maybe.

There was a lot about IVF that we hadn't known before. I'd never looked into it, always so hopeful that we would get pregnant like everyone else. But now that we were on the precipice of the next stage of our IVF journey, I re-examined the stats we'd been given and baulked. Those undergoing IVF who are aged thirty-four or under, as I was, had a 32 per cent chance of having a live birth per embryo transferred, which

I was so shocked at. Surely that's not a great figure? If I were told that my brain surgery only had a 32 per cent success rate, I might look at other options. The older the mother, the smaller the chance becomes: between ages thirty-five and thirty-seven, the percentage dropped to 25; at thirty-eight and thirty-nine, the chances were 19 per cent; forty to forty-two was 11 per cent and over forty-two wasn't recommended, as the success was under 5 per cent.

I thought about the day in some blurry future when everything finally worked out for us; when I would hold those little fingers between mine in the fluorescent lights of the hospital suite where it was impossible to tell whether it was day or night-time. Would our future baby be older than the other babies on the ward somehow? They would have metamorphosed from an older egg, one with near 'geriatric' DNA and all the pain of my lived experience stored up there inside its gossamer walls. Would my baby be born with wrinkles already stamped into its brow? Or maybe the eyes of an old soul to navigate its life? Was I old enough now to be a mother? Had I atoned and paid the price for whatever the gods had punished me for?

Yes, I was thirty-four with my 32 per cent chance for a positive IVF cycle, the highest it could possibly be, but the pressure was on.

Egg retrieval day comes around and I am shaking with giddiness in the back of the early-morning taxi down to Wilmslow. The process is like going into surgery – I am put under for the twenty-minute procedure and wake up feeling like I've just had the best night's sleep of my life, one that may or may not have involved alien abduction. Lying in the recovery room in my backless gown, I find out that of my dozens of eggs that have grown in size from the hormonal stimulation, only nine could be harvested. Of the nine, only five were viable. Of the five, only four had fertilised. At this point of the process, the fertilised eggs are given a few days to incubate and form 'blastocysts', the next step on the journey.

Waiting is the absolute worst.

I get updates from the lab on days one, three and five about how our little blastocysts are doing. But by day five, I am told that of the four fertilised eggs, only one of our embryos has survived.

'It's a low-grade embryo,' the embryologist tells me in a flat, tired voice over the phone. 'A 4CC minus, which means it hasn't quite broken out of its shell but it's still viable. Just about.' They have given it an extra day just to see if it will improve but after today they will have to discard our little blastocyst if we decide not to use it. 'Shall we give it a go?'

I shrug into the phone, my heart on the floor. Well, *I* don't know, do I? Do low-grade embryos sometimes stick? What percentage chance does it have? I'm up to my eyeballs in progesterone at this point – like PMT but for weeks on end – and barely know my own name.

'Yes,' I squeak. 'Let's do it.'

We had one chance and I was going to take it.

I kept reminding myself of the blackbird with its message of change and transformation. And then of the hare – a symbol of fertility – leading me into the unknown. What bigger, more unknown transformation could there possibly be than motherhood?

The 'putting it back in' process is a bit simpler than the harvest but we have been delayed. Due to the barrage of drugs and who knows what else (my delicate disposition, perhaps?), my ovaries have swollen up to what feels like twice their normal size because of a condition that is commonplace with IVF called Ovarian Hyperstimulation Syndrome. No one seems particularly concerned but my ovaries feel like they are trying to push up and form a new landmark outside of my skin so we have to wait another month for the 'embryo transfer' procedure. I suppose it's sensible but it means being pumped full of hormones to prepare my womb lining for another thirty days. In this time, our little Day Six blastocyst is frozen and I sit at home thinking wistfully of my potential child sitting icy and alone forty miles away from me in Wilmslow.

When the day finally comes, I lie with my knees bunched around my ears and my hair in a gauzy net back in the operating theatre. Will holds my hand with both of his, looking studiously at the screen in his own funny cap and gown.

'And I'm inserting the embryo – now.'

We watch the ultrasound monitor as the doctor pops our little embryo in place in a dazzling flash of white light. A celestial explosion. Does all life look this way when it forms – an angelic glow momentarily lighting up our insides as souls cross over from the other side and start to snuggle into the red-velvet folds of the womb? Now, wouldn't that be a beautiful thing? I smile at the screen, seeing our minuscule blastocyst sitting there in my thick, doughy womb lining that I've spent so long making cosy for it.

Be safe, little one. We're ready for you, 4CC minus. Be strong for us.

And then, we're done.

The rules for afterward are pretty straightforward: rest, rest and more rest. Keep your ankles warm – a tenet of Traditional Chinese Medicine that everyone on their TTC journey knows – take your vitamin D and folic acid. No jumping, no flailing your legs in the air. Just sit down – yes, right there – and let your womb (and the fresh round of tablets and pessaries) do their work.

We get food on the way home, me with my warm, fluffy socks shoved into my trainers in the middle of Pizza Express as we natter, letting out all of that anticipation and nervous energy. I get a parking ticket but it doesn't seem to matter on this glorious day with its celestial light still shining inside me.

And then the two-week wait commences.

My world has become small again. But instead of grieving, my days are filled with waiting. I hadn't counted on there being more than one way I could go out of my mind but here I am, back on the sofa, agog at the most tedious year known to humankind. When the weekend comes around, I'm desperate for any excuse to leave the house, in spite of the fatigue that hits me in heavy ocean rolls, so Will and I are now admiring the lavender stacked up outside in the sunny supermarket car park.

'This will go perfectly in the Sky Garden!' I say. 'How many shall we get?'

'I'm not sure. Maybe five?'

I look at him sideways to check he isn't joking then begin to load up the basket with as much lavender as we can carry (in my delicate condition).

I reach out to sweep in more lavender pots when I see the smudge mark on my hand. Wait, not a smudge – a ladybird!

'Will!'

Tears immediately start to blur my vision. Damn you, progesterone. I don't have to whir my Rolodex of symbolism too hard as I know exactly what the ladybird means.

We both stare at the back of my hand in the car park, the sound of trolleys clattering in our ears. The ladybird is as inconspicuous as a beauty mark just under my right thumb but every spot glistens with meaning.

This was not the first time this had happened. In fact, a ladybird had also landed on my hand in June 2023 – one month before we found out we were pregnant with Sky.

'Let's see, shall we?' Will says softly and smiles gently at me.

I nod, reverent.

After another moment, I lean down to the lavender bushes but the ladybird is staying firmly put – its six little feet are fastened to my pores and its white eyes are blissfully vacant as if it is having a whale of a time feeling a different texture under its feet.

'Well,' I say, 'I guess it's coming inside to do the Big Shop with us.' I cup my other hand around it like I'm holding the remains of a small star.

While not explicitly a symbol of fertility, ladybirds are historic symbols of good luck, transformation and new beginnings – their shining red bodies seen not as signs of warning but of a pulsing lifeforce and vitality, sprinkling luck on the hands of maidens. In Britain, there is a longstanding tradition that if a ladybird lands on the hand of a young woman, she will soon be married. I can't profess to be overly young or very single, but I'm hoping this correlates to another kind of new beginning.

In European folklore, ladybirds were often linked with the Virgin Mary, with their name deriving from 'Our Lady's bird'. The red of their wings was said to represent Mary's cloak, while their seven spots were thought to symbolise her seven joys and seven sorrows. As a result, farmers in the medieval period believed ladybirds were a divine gift, sent to protect crops from pests, and would pray to the Virgin Mary's helper to keep those pesky aphids away. In parts of Eastern Europe, ladybirds were seen as messengers from the heavens, carrying prayers to the gods or bringing down blessings from the skies, while some beliefs thought that ladybirds could predict the weather – if they flew high, good weather would follow; if they stayed low, storms were on the horizon.

When I was little, there was a 'ladybird summer' where you couldn't move for round red beetles. They could cluster on my grandparents' conifer trees, shining like rubies in the baking sun. We'd encourage them onto our little fingers, wrinkling our noses at the minuscule pebbles of golden ladybird poop they left behind. If you were quiet, with the sun on your face, they would remain on your fingers for long minutes until those ungainly grey translucent wings flared out to carry them away.

Yes, I think about this but I also think of the ladybird that refused to leave my hand on that early summer day last year.

What is around the corner for us next month?

I carry the ladybird through the fruit and veg, down the tin aisle and over to the tills, my hand held rigid so it keeps its perch on me like a stunning bird of paradise. Of course, I realise I am just a silly millennial woman with a ladybird on her hand in the middle of Lidl but it feels important that I see this beautiful beetle to safety.

'Back in a minute,' I say to Will and take the ladybird through the checkouts.

Outside again, away from the synthetic chill of the freezers, I hold my hand up to the sun and watch that tangle of silver wings flip out, carrying all my hopes with them.

'See you soon,' I whisper.

Later on, I am lying on the patio with the Sky Garden all around me. I lift up my shirt to press my hand to my belly and close my eyes. It is rounded with bloating from all the treatment and the constant poking and prodding. I know this but that distended curve is disconcerting to me. I feel like I'm already three months pregnant – if only.

'Hello?' I whisper.

I get a big, loud nothing back.

I wouldn't talk to my neighbours if I was still moving in my furniture either. *I'll cut you some slack, 4CC minus.*

There is buzzing all around me, the sounds of a dozen insects, but there are no ladybirds on the lavender quite yet. Soon though. I myself am buzzing with excitement in my tight cocoon of waiting.

I wake Will up at five a.m. after a restless night. The moment is finally here and I am quivering from head to toe.

We wait, hands over our mouths. The bathroom light flickers. We look down at the test.

One line appears.

Just one.

Negative.

I squint harder, thinking I must still be dreaming, my eyes half pasted together with sleep.

Negative. No. How could this be?

'I don't understand,' I say as Will wraps me into his chest. My arms feel like they're made of rubber as I attempt to clasp him back. The test is negative. All that physical torment, all that emotional turmoil, all those thousands of pounds worth of debt, only to find no little orange seed waiting inside me. My insides hold nothing whatsoever except the heaviness of dying tissue getting ready to be shed. I want to grab Will by the upper arms and scream at him, 'But we saw the ladybird! It was a sign!'

The signs had told me good luck was right around the corner.

But the signs have also driven me half mad.

How many more fertile hares, mysterious blackbirds and fairy-like ladybirds do I have to behold before I finally realise that nothing is coming for me? Nothing. No baby. Those symbols were meant for someone else standing right behind me and I had waved at them frantically, thinking they were speaking to me.

That desperate feeling is back – the one I had felt in the hospital during Sky's many ultrasounds. The one I had felt all those months of peeing on sticks and receiving a blank space. Maybe it really is a trick this time though. What if the clinic had told me to test too early? What if I am actually pregnant and it's just not showing up yet? What if, what if, what if?

Please, please let this be the case.

But a few days later, I'm sitting on the sofa with a piece of cake in my hand. I'm nodding with approval over this slice of heaven I've just welcomed into my mouth, ready to put on an obligatory episode of *The Office*, when suddenly my body goes numb. It's like someone has forced a block of ice into my mouth and I feel its cold heaviness travel down my throat and intestines, hitting my stomach's floor like a brick. Something doesn't feel right and is not the cake.

It is a deep and yearning sadness.

Maybe I just need to sleep it off, I think, pulling on my cosiest pyjamas even though it is only mid-morning and I have just showered. I grab my blue rabbit and go to bed. Then something in my uterus drops.

I start to bleed. Profusely.

No.

No. No. No. No.

The test was right. It wasn't a trick. I realise then how much hope I'd been holding on to, wishing I could be the exception, the one in a million. But really I am still the one in 5,000.

Not another month. I can't go another month without being pregnant. I'm in shock. I am home alone, bleeding and bleeding out another month of stored-up hope.

And with that, the tears return as my whole world implodes.

There have been many times over the past few months when I've thought that death wouldn't be such a bad option. A bit of a reprieve from all this thick mourning fog. I'd read Dolores Cannon's *Between Death and Life* and harvested all the information I could about life after death. I think back to all of the near-death experience videos I'd clocked up online directly after Sky's passing; middle-aged women telling a podcast camera about how they floated out of their bodies and calmly watched the scene of an accident play out below them before zipping upwards towards a light where all their favourite people were waiting for them. Seeing Sky, Grandma and Grandad again – now wouldn't that be nice?

There were times in my fugue state back in winter this year when I'd almost skip my meds. Maybe the sepsis would come roaring back and drag me under like a silver, mercurial sea. I would release a deep exhale and see something shining above me, hear a calming voice then begin to feel weightless.

Right now, the feeling comes back again. The words, 'Wow, I can't wait to die.'

The road of infertility is a lonely, lightless place but I never ever thought this journey would lead me here.

I am angry that this hasn't been easy. That nothing feels like it has ever been easy – I take stock of my life and get swept under by a tide of struggling. The constant health battles from the time I was thirteen, the bullies, the abusive ex-boyfriends, the severe, debilitating social anxiety and depression that have held me back from most things in my life. Now there's just another thing to add to the list of things that I'm not good at. Can't be happy, can't hold down a job, can't understand social cues, can't keep my husband by my side because I'm so fucking sad my baby died, can't have a healthy baby, can't stop crying. But also – can't read the signs.

It is 9:56 a.m.

I crawl back into bed and begin the long, arduous wait for Will to return home from work.

Needless to say, this was not the finish line.

Chapter Ten

Deer

In pregnancy, we are steered away from the stats. 'Don't google anything,' is the standard statement thrown around by midwives, ultrasound technicians and doctors. Instead, the pastel-coloured baby books teach us about hypnobirthing, vitamins, breathing techniques, birthing pools and cosy mummy groups. But they forget to mention the rest. You will not find your very worst nightmares in the pages of a baby book.

The charity Tommy's, however, does not shy away from the stark facts. Its website reads:

> Our mission is to make the UK the safest place in the world to give birth. In the UK, it is estimated that 1 in 4 pregnancies end in loss during pregnancy or birth. 53,000 babies are born prematurely. We research causes and treatments so we can make pregnancy and birth safer for all.

One in four. One in *four*. Twenty-five per cent.

The figure encompasses miscarriages, stillbirths, chemical pregnancies and termination for medical reasons (TFMR).

I spoke with a dear friend recently who lost her little boy at fourteen weeks, a few weeks after we lost Sky. She said that her consultant revealed that the most recent figure was actually closer to one in three.

At the time I was pregnant, there were five of us in the same boat. Four friends and I who were pregnant at the same time, clearing Tesco out of ginger-nut biscuits and winching our eyelids open at two p.m. every day. I was excited to be going through this life-altering experience with so many of my closest friends and I eagerly awaited their WhatsApps of bump updates ('Which fruit are you today, girl?'), while stockpiling baby-shower presents under my bed. But out of the five of us, only two of those babies survived to be born alive – two lost to second-trimester miscarriages and Sky, who was terminated for medical reasons four weeks before I hit my third trimester – and this was just amongst my small friendship group. Perhaps the stats are higher even than the latest figures.

At the hospital, they gave Will and me a beautiful memory box for Sky; somewhere for us to keep her footprints and the replica of the teddy that would be in her coffin. After all, she had no other possessions other than what I had filled her nursery with – the homemade cat rattle from a friend, the teddies with the fur so soft they were like velveteen clouds and the pinewood cot bought second-hand from Facebook Marketplace much too early on in my pregnancy. The box was a pale yellow-cream, about as big as a large shoebox, and covered – once again – in those mysterious purple butterflies. Inside, we found they had recorded her birth time wrong on the fake hospital bracelet they had supplied and, at that, I absolutely lost my shit.

'What's this?' I said, as I unrolled an A6 scroll tied with a gold plastic band. It was a certificate.

A blank certificate.

Name.

Place of birth.

Time of birth.

All the fields were blank.

'What the...' I threw it down, the tears seeming to spring out of me, as if until that moment I'd been holding my thumb inside a beer barrel to staunch the flow.

A keepsake record of my daughter's life. A blank certificate that no medical professional was legally required to fill out.

'It's not even filled in! They didn't even fucking fill it in!' I threw it onto the bed and began to howl as Will stared at me wide-eyed. Linnet turned up her purr dial to full.

I had known that she was classed as too young to be added to any official register. I couldn't nip to the registry office and watch them write down her name in neat, careful curves. And yet, she had been legally too old for the standard termination process. I had birthed her. I had seen her, I had held her, I had smelled her head and kissed her soft cheek. It was as cold as it might have been from a chilly walk in the park.

She was not recorded anywhere. No one would ever know her name.

Since starting to write this book, the law has changed and now bereaved parents can apply for a Baby Loss Certificate. On 22nd February 2024, a gov.uk press release said: 'Parents who have experienced the devastation of losing a baby before 24 weeks of pregnancy can apply for a certificate to have their grief recognised from today.' Initially given to those who had experienced their loss after September 2018, the date has since been amended to encompass all pregnancy losses. You can guarantee that I applied for my certificate the morning applications began.

What a sincere joy it is to have this acknowledgement. Until you have planned out a birth, a name and a life for someone, you may never know how important it feels to have a marker for this kind of loss. Many people like me who have lost a much-wanted baby are expected to just 'get on with it' after the most poignant event of their lives, with the grief of so many women and parents brushed under the rug.

The TV presenter and politician Baroness Floella Benjamin (whom I remember fondly from my early '90s children's telly) has herself experienced three miscarriages and said:

> We and the millions of other bereaved parents have been waiting to be recognised to understand the grief we have gone through. I still feel it. Not everyone will want it but to some people it will be something to treasure ... I will be celebrating when I get my certificate of loss.[19]

There is so much power in acknowledgement.

Because of the absolute shitshow going on in the US since the overturning of Roe v. Wade and the surprise appearance of the second Trump administration, I often think about what might have happened if we had lived over the water. Had I been forced to carry my pregnancy to term and deliver a baby not compatible with life, I wonder about what my mental state might be at this time; how much longer my recovery and how much greater my sense of loss. The UK's Baby Loss Certificate, on the other hand, feels like such a kind gesture to all those grieving parents who have all been through the worst pain known to humankind.

I spoke to my mum and the mums of my friends about it. They all said, 'This never happened when we were young. What do you think is causing this epidemic of baby loss? Microplastics? Vaccines?' But as time went on, the stories came out. They had known someone who had had a miscarriage. A friend of a friend whose son was stillborn but no one ever said his name again. When we first began to tell people about what had happened to us, we were met with a surprising – and shocking – outpouring of stories. Friends, family members and colleagues all came forward to tell us that they or a close friend had been through the same experience – or if not this specific one then something incredibly similar. We heard tearful tales of repeated miscarriage, ectopic pregnancy, neonatal deaths and abnormalities that meant very sick babies were terminated for medical reasons. We absorbed the shockwaves of each story, buried down and hidden from society – these were people we had known for years, but why hadn't we ever heard these stories before? These things are happening every single day, but this kind of grief – the pain of losing someone you had never met – is not part of our consciousness. It is not that these things didn't happen in 1960 or 1990, it's just that 'it wasn't spoken about back then'.

But I'm speaking about it. I want to talk about the mind-bending grief that is affecting families behind all those red-brick facades. I want to talk about all the little lives that didn't make it to their first smile. I want to talk about my Sky.

I want to talk about her. All. The. Time.

No one asks about her anymore but I will always say her name.

Lammas arrives and the constant summer rain lifts to blue skies and clean, full-bodied air.

On the morning of the first of August, I sit outside with my cup of tea, watching every creature my garden has ever hosted zipping along the fence, hovering above the shaggy grass and tweeting all over the birdfeeder. It is barely eight a.m. but the sound of the bees gathering near the sweet-scented apple tree has me raising my face to the easterly air and humming my own form of praise to Mother Nature.

It's hard to be suicidal when there's a chiffchaff singing in the willows and swifts are screeching overhead. Believe me, I've tried.

Lammas is the first harvest festival of the year. Also known as Lughnasadh, the Pagan sabbat is a celebration of the first crops – the bursting tomatoes, the carrots, the furry cucumbers and the peppers – and allows us time to give thanks for all that we have, throwing our hands up to the beating sun. Gratitude and harvest are a huge part of the Pagan Wheel of the Year – we are only a few generations removed from when the crop cycles would have dominated our worldview – but in more recent times, due to our lack of handiness with a scythe, Lammas has become more of a cerebral festival, making us take stock of the things we value in our lives – our own personal, inner harvest – including our communities and connection with the Earth.

Much like Beltane, Samhain and Imbolc, Lammas is another of the cross-quarter days, so it packs a big magic-laced punch and has legends of its own. According to Irish myth, Tailtiu was an Earth goddess known for her fertility and nurturing qualities, particularly when it came to farming. She toiled tirelessly, tilling the soil and making way for crops to grow. However, her efforts took a toll on her, and she eventually collapsed from exhaustion and passed away.

To honour Tailtiu's memory, Lugh – the famed god of light and harvest as well as being Tailtiu's foster son – established the festival of Lughnasadh (shame he didn't use his foster mum's name instead, right?). The celebration included festivities, games, competitions and feasting and was honoured by the people of the land, who viewed this time as one of both gratitude and preparation for the coming autumn and winter months.

The apples on our tree are tingling with freshness – just another month until we can finally pick them after weeks of tantalisation. In fact, everything is bursting with sweetness.

Almost everything.

I balance my own roster of gratitude:

I am grateful for my incredible family and friends. I am grateful for my home and my peace. I am grateful for Will and for Linnet. And I am grateful to be sitting in my beautiful garden right now.

It's best to keep the list small this year.

I look down and catch a male orange-tipped butterfly scouting out my lawn for cuckoo flowers. It finds one and hangs upside down like a featherweight monkey on the pale, fairy-like flower. I watch transfixed.

A butterfly.

Hope has entered the chat once again.

No, I say. Don't listen to that voice.

I have only just started venturing outside again after my breakdown. Following my descent into IVF darkness, I had hidden myself away from everyone and anyone, wearing the covers over my head like a midwinter bonnet. Fertility and getting pregnant again were all I could think about. I lived and breathed vitamins and basal body temperatures to mask the fact of my reality: I was thirty-four, childless and barely existing. I was playing dangerously with hope. I tempted it to thread my body with gold again, only for the stitches to fall apart twenty-eight days later.

To counter the swarming thoughts of actual, clinical insanity, I relied heavily on sunshine and learning Stoic phrases by rote:

'Cease to hope and you will cease to fear.'

'The whole future lies in uncertainty: live immediately.'

'The mind that is anxious about future events is miserable.'

While Seneca might not be a jovial sort of bloke, he has some corkers if you want to live your life without constant disappointment. If you expect nothing and just crack on with living a life that makes you happy and where you do good by others, then what could go wrong?

The butterfly patters away, finding footholds in the air. This isn't the only butterfly I've seen this week. Not a sign. Just an indicator of two people not cutting the lawn to let the wildflowers grow.

Over the past couple of weeks, I have been coming to terms with perhaps the biggest realisation of my adult life:

Maybe the symbols don't mean anything, after all.

There it is – rocking my most firmly held belief.

In all honesty, how much longer can I carry on this journey of searching for deeper meaning if the signs were never pointing me in the right direction? Or maybe they were never there in the first place?

What would Epictetus say? Probably something like, 'Who gives a shit? We're all going to die soon anyway.' However, I'm finding it so difficult to detach from my hard-wired Pagan roots, especially when the world looks beautiful enough to have been made by design. To distance myself from nature's symbols is to go against everything I have felt with a resounding truth in my life and to defy my Pagan path.

How can I remain a Pagan if I've noted the signs of fertility yet have no positive pregnancy test to act as proof? Is there a way I can still worship the Earth but close off my eyes and ears to her many messages? Maybe, but would the path now be shaded instead of lit by full sun?

With these discomforting thoughts, I couldn't feel any less like myself.

So, it is time for me to take a short madness interlude and touch grass.

In my wild little garden, the cherry tree flourishes – a symbol of hope, purity and youth. Three months ago, its branches were spilling over with blossom. The golden motes of pollen drifted over the bee boxes and the wildflowers on the lawn, hazing up my vision and filling me up to my teeth with verdant sweetness. I watched transfixed as the overfilled branches swayed in the breeze, feeling hypnotised by spring. Now, the tree's first fruits have revealed themselves. They came overnight; rock-hard green kernels appearing in a flash, popping out of the ether. Very soon, these tough knots will become glossy, purple cherries, their juices running thickly into the grass as a sweet offering to the worms below.

Amongst the cherry tree's greenery are the two vibrant blue ribbons with their messages of hope and remembrance. They flutter gently above as I sit cross-legged below and close my eyes. I begin to feel into the world – stretching out that cobweb of my unseen consciousness to touch all that is visible and veiled. It does not take me long to feel what I am looking for.

The Earth Elementals. The spirits of the land.

They are here all around me. I have never seen one, only felt them. They are tricky to lay eyes on and their only scents are wet earth and warm August grass. But they – the gnomes and small earth-dwellers – feel like soft fingers holding your hair out of your face when you bend low to examine a stud of tormentil. Or like the earth pushing back against your bare toes as you press them into the soil. They do not reside in every patch of land: the Elementals dwell in places where the land is loved and cared for, just those areas that are sacred and tended by the trees; the places adored by the sparrows, the deer and the tiniest shrews. Perhaps the Earth Elementals are attracted to the places that emit a steady beacon of calm, just as we humans exhale deeply when we see an opening in the tree canopy or hear a blackbird after the rain. They are perhaps just like us.

This is the first time I've felt them in my garden and I feel a surge of pride well up in me.

I'm struggling to understand how these can be real and the symbols I've seen are not. Right now, I feel the Earth Elementals around me. The air feels thick with voices and hands around my body; the welcome press of magic enfolds me. I watch the ribbons fluttering, wondering if the movement is an Earth spirit's doing or only the slight breeze rippling iridescent in the sunshine. I tilt my head up and say:

'Guardians of the Earth and Land,
Bless me with your steady hand.
From soil and stone, your power flows,
Keep me strong and help me grow.'

The cherry tree's leaves flutter in acknowledgement of my simple healing prayer, and I wonder if there is another spirit amongst them today – a spirit kind and gentle, good as gold, and small enough to fit in the crook of my arm.

I still haven't felt her and suppose I never will now.

People, with all their wisdom, tell me her spirit is still around me but who am I to say? You'd think a mother would be able to feel her child near always. But maybe Sky never stayed around after I felt her go in that hospital room; maybe she had another bigger, more important purpose waiting for her outside of the warm cage of my arms and the confines of her carefully chosen name.

The thought is comforting and heartbreaking all at once.

I get up and feel all my joints click into place. The cherry tree looks so merry in all its black-blooded finery. I face the tree and say the words: 'That's it now. That is enough grief.'

The time has finally come.

I need to get my life back. It is a reluctant pull to the real world but it is there, nonetheless. My heart feels green-plated with healing; all the woven strands of my nature walks have plugged into each vital organ and shocked them back to life in a pulsewave of limes, emeralds and jades. Or has it been my writing? Did I reform my body and mind by writing this book and getting all those crumbled thoughts out onto the page to be absorbed into syntax and serif fonts? Or maybe it was just the passage of sunlit time.

Whatever the reason, I start seeing a therapist.

I find Jo on a counselling directory website. No matter how many times I scroll through the pages and pages of faces and indecipherable qualifications, I keep coming back to her. Amongst her specialities are baby loss and infertility, and while there are a lot of therapists who specialise in these things, there's something about Jo – with her smiling but still serious face and long auburn hair – that makes me feel safe and held, even before I've met her. We arrange a quick call for that day and I just know that I've made the right choice. She is based in Southend-on-Sea, so is clearly quite confused to hear my Lancashire tones. What drew me to her? Perhaps yet another instance of fate, but this time for all the right reasons.

Over the years, I've been quite the therapeutic connoisseur and will rave to just about anyone on the benefits of letting all that pent-up emotion out through talking. That is not to say it is easy and I'm aware I have quite the fresh trauma under my belt.

Poor Jo, I think as I log into Zoom for our first session.

'Take your time, Jenn.'

My body is twisted into a pretzel as I tell her everything – hands melded together in my lap and legs double-wrapped in an impressive double-jointed feat. I am coiled like a DNA helix with all my words trapped in that tight spiral. Even recounting the facts now, almost eight months on, is viscerally painful and makes a noise well up above my diaphragm that is definitely not human. But in spite of the pain, I have come here for a reason and we talk about everything openly and frankly. What other way is there to be? There is no use being selective and I let it all out: the smell of our mingled bloods, the slight peeling of her skin away from the tender soles of her feet, the sense – even now – that I have lost the most precious things in my life.

But laid out on the table like that, it all seems a bit much.

'I mean,' I say, forcing a bright smile, 'I know I have so many wonderful things in my life. I have an amazing family, truly, and I have a beautiful house. We are absolutely fine.'

Jo frowns but nods. 'It sounds like you don't feel entitled to make a fuss about this.'

I stumble. 'I just want to acknowledge... ' I trail off, unsure what I'm trying to say.

'I wonder how difficult it would be for you to verbalise how truly challenging this experience has been for you. Yes, there are so many *other* horrors in the world that you haven't been through but you have been through *this* horror and it is one that is still affecting you. You have been through a trauma, Jenn.'

There are no 'at leasts'.

Something untwists in me. Of course the loss of her has been dreadful – I can't imagine going through anything more painful in my life, barring the loss of more loved ones. Of course it is taking me so long to feel like me again: everything in my life has changed.

'I don't understand it,' I say, trying to keep the petulance from my voice. 'We're doing everything right. We did everything right. I've always done everything right.'

'Do you want to tell me a little more about that?'

I twist my hands and look away from the screen. As I try to think about how I've been feeling, it comes out in a tumble as something like this:

'I'm a practising Pagan and, as part of that, I believe strongly that everything in this world is fated and written in the stars in the dome of the Universe. Therefore, I believe that what has happened to us was fated and some kind of punishment for something I have done. I have been trying to atone; checking a list of karmic checkboxes, healing myself and getting myself into the best place I could possibly be to become a mother again. If I did all this and met all the criteria, I would be let off the hook and chosen again. But nothing has happened, I'm still not a mother to a living child, even though I'm trying so, so hard and this has been going on for so long. I try so hard every day that it's exhausting. And I'm frustrated, my god, I'm frustrated. I look around at the world and see everyone else just living their lives, doing terrible things to those around them and to the planet we all live on. They are not atoning, they are not serving the world. Maybe it'll take some cataclysmic event for them to go on their own karmic journey. But here I am – stuck. Stuck with no baby, stuck having to witness everything wrong with this world because I have this knowledge now; a knowing of what happens when we get on the bad side of fate.'

There is a heavy beat of silence while Jo sets her mouth, preparing a question that may crush or heal me.

'Jenn,' she looks pensive. 'What does relinquishing control look like to you?'

I pause.

There is a heavy weight in my chest that rumbles and groans.

'I'm someone who likes to control everything in my life,' I admit. 'I've spent so long controlling other people's perceptions of me that I'm frustrated when I can't control everything around me, or when people are not controlling themselves in the same rigid way I am. Why are they not trying when I have to try this hard for something I so desperately want? I can't control our fertility and the knowledge of that is killing me inside.'

Perspective really is everything.

These sessions are not the place for lies, even if the truth seems like 'too much'. Everything I have always done is tied so thoroughly to control. Perhaps that is the lesson that this was all trying to teach me. *Sky, did our paths really have to be so difficult just to open my eyes?*

What would it feel like to let go? To tap the tight fist in my chest and force it to open? To finally surrender to the possibility that motherhood will come in its own sweet time or never at all?

I realise I have absolutely no idea.

After the session, I take the day slowly. Everything feels different under my new lens.

Evening arrives and I feel freer and heavier all at once. I pull out the sofa bed in the spare room once again and lie down to watch the sky pinkening over the orange-tiled roofs and the tips of the willow tree behind our fence. The sky has the iridescent shimmer that can only come on warm summer nights – as if it were already in the process of making someone's childhood memories shine. My house backs onto a large open playing field so that the sky always looks so wide and rolling above us and, at this time of year, I can see all the way over to the hillside moors. They are beginning to turn purple with heather blooms so that the air is sweet and thick with the scent of wild honey.

Linnet hops up and stretches out on her side next to me, looking like a chocolate-coated boomerang.

'I'm knackered, Lin.'

She slow-blinks at me, pink nose raised.

'If only you wouldn't maul me to death if I asked for a cuddle.'

I am looking at the purple and orange edges of the clouds when a shaft of colour reaches me. I raise up off my elbows, eyes fixed.

A rainbow.

Well, would you look at that!

I can only see the upward shard of the rainbow's tail over the suburban houses on the other side of the park. It is not lost on me that a baby born to someone after loss is called a 'rainbow baby', with rainbows being ubiquitous symbols of hope; sun through the drizzle. What a little slice of magic to see on a beautiful August evening. There isn't even any rain...

The rainbow fades and I bask in its residual glitter.

I turn eagerly, keen to get her opinion. 'Did you see that, Lin? What did you think of that?'

A white-tipped tail swishes back and forth.

But then I'm at my window again. What is *that*?

'What?'

A roe deer is standing behind my garden fence.

There's a deer at the bottom of my garden!

I feel like I've just stumbled into a Barbie movie. All that I need now is a unicorn, brought here by the flourished tip of another rainbow. What the hell is a deer doing here? I've never seen deer anywhere near my home and yet there it is, a young stag chowing down on the brambles behind my fence. My face is split into the widest grin I have felt all year.

Gentleness, compassion, wisdom and fertility. Deer are long-held symbols of all that is good in the world. Open any book of Arthurian legend and there are deer all over the place leading you to mysterious and beautiful glades, ready to show you your potent destiny. In some Scottish communities, deer were called 'fairy cattle' and the Ancient Celtic people saw them as magical creatures that could slip between worlds; their knock-knees trembling over the threshold to the human lands.

But I am not allowed to believe in those things anymore, as such ideas only cause more pain. There are few things I can control in this world, and a baby does not seem to be one of them, even if the signs do keep telling me that good, fertile and joyous things are to come. Where are they then? Do I have to seek the bottom of another rainless rainbow? Or do I just have to surrender and wait for my blessing to arrive? These mixed messages are exhausting and I resolve that the Universe knows absolutely nothing whatsoever and can jump in the sea.

Where has this deer come from though? Has it really fallen off a sky-arched bridge and landed at the bottom of my garden to give me a message?

Not at all. I live in an area where deer are plentiful, getting shunted around the countryside as their habitats are turned over to soulless new developments, displaced and homesick. It is perhaps less well known that a large deer population is a sign of an imbalance in the countryside, just as too many humans are the sign of an imbalanced world. On my daily walks, I see fawns flourishing, caught in glimpses between the spindly legs of their mothers. This one is a young stag, perhaps only a year old and heading into the first rutting season of its life. I cast my eyes around for any sign of its mother or herd but there are no other dun or russet bodies amongst the bramble hedge. Roe deer, once into adulthood, are mainly solitary creatures throughout the warmer months, forming loose groups during winter, only staying with their mothers for around twelve months.

While the rut – or deer breeding season – happens between July and August, the female's fertilised egg doesn't implant until the following January, which is quite a talent. No doe wants to be pregnant in the harsh northern winter, of course. Once the strongest females have survived, implantation occurs, with gestation lasting five months until those little dappled darlings are born in May–June time, camouflaged by their speckled coats. Roe females aren't exactly hooves-on parents, returning to their offspring several times a day to let them suckle but otherwise leaving them unguarded in the tall grass.

Those first summer months are tough, with some studies putting the infant mortality rate at 52 per cent in the two months after birth. Sadly, this is due mainly to fox predation, disease, hypothermia, starvation and grass mowing. It is no wonder that mothers have developed a way to keep predators at bay by steering clear of their offspring and drawing attention away.

Many years ago, when I lived in Lancaster, my housemate and I would walk on summer evenings, jumping in the car after work, cramming sandwiches into our faces as we rode away from the city centre so as not to waste a single moment of daylight. We arrived at our destination usually just after six-thirty. Even then, before the peak of midsummer, there were still hours of sunshine left to go and I held out my forearms to watch them glow.

The wood we had in our sights was not on the path of dog walkers or rock climbers on their way to the crags but was nestled in a stout valley, shaded on all sides from the harsh coastal weather by green hills. It was so hidden that I believed it might stand empty of human life for many days at a time, left only to the devices of skittering willow tits and prowling mink. This had given it time to grow wild. Underfoot lay swathes of unbroken moss banks, so bright with life they looked like they'd been coloured in with a child's felt-tip pen. Tree pollen floated in the shards of light above the greenery and, in this mystical undercover world, it was not hard to see how stories of fairies, imps and other realms had first come into being. Growing up, I'd read my mum's old 1970s picture book of *The Grimm's Fairy Tales*, obscure stories I've never heard since, ones that had yet to be canonised by Disney. This wood might have held the twisted tower where a princess spun capes out of nettles to free her brothers who had been turned into swans. No one would find her here. Or the hut in the forest where the old, bewitched man with his animal servants lay in wait for lost little girls.

'I've got goosebumps,' I laughed. 'Look.'

My housemate and I walked and talked, chattering in a way that did not belong in the woods, poking our 'mopey thighs' that had not yet seen enough hills that year and plotting our next expedition, even though this one had barely started. But we showed our respect for the place in other ways, running our hands over gouges in the tree bark and stopping to admire swirls of bright lichen on half-disintegrated boundary walls. 'Ooh, nice bit of moss, that.'

My phone tucked neatly in my rucksack, I hadn't been keeping an eye on the time. The contrast of heat and shade had fooled me into thinking this was the middle of the day and that the woods were ours for another few hours yet. The world around us quickly descended into a twilight realm. Goose pimples peppered the sides of my calves and I immediately grabbed my elbows like I was Snow White surrounded by the bright eyes of unseen creatures. We were in the heart of the woods, nowhere near the rim – we could have been in any northern European forest after dark, in any period of history – and, in the gloom and sudden chill, I wished I could speed through a million years of evolution and develop echolocation.

And then I heard it.

It was a sound so uncanny I felt my blood congeal into icy slivers. The noise was a cross between an enraged dog and metal tearing. I looked at where the opaque outline of my friend stood beside me and I caught the last speckles of light in the white curve of his eyes. Neither of us moved.

Again, there it was. The sound thundered out – it couldn't have been further than twenty metres away – the harsh notes glancing off the edges of trees to where we stood, dark spindles rooted to the ground.

'What is that?' he breathed.

While the word 'demon' flashed before my eyes and the darkness rolled in around me, I knew the real answer: 'Deer. Let's go.' Pebbles and roots scattered and tugged as we fled to the tree line; the faint light there beckoning us like a singed white flag.

Out in the open fields once more, the evening was lit by stars that hadn't been visible below the canopy. The yellow glow of two farmhouses over on the far side of the paddock seemed to slow my breathing, which I hadn't realised was a little ragged up until that point. At that moment, I wasn't sure if I was being warned away from the woods by a beloved woodland creature or something ancient whose name had not been spoken in many centuries.

The whole thing felt like something out of the gothic novels I consumed as a teenager, hell-bent on the thrill of melodrama and the threat of the night. Horace Walpole's cursed castle corridors and the corrupt monk Ambrosio's pact with the Devil kept me reading late into the night. Wrapped in a literary world of carefully constructed fear, every shape and creak could be a potential demon in disguise or a ghost that would haunt my insomniac nights for years to come. We hadn't seen what we had heard in the woods. Perhaps the earth had opened up from the base of a black-mottled oak and birthed the monsters we'd been taught about as children. The boggarts, the kelpies, the bogeyman. Or maybe this was a new breed altogether.

We scurried back to Lancaster, laughing nervously all the way back in the car, as if we couldn't quite shake off the echo of the beast until we were back safe in our riverside flat.

This was not the first time I had heard the frantic shout of a female deer desperate to defend its young. *Get out. Get out of this place. You are in my domain.* The first time I was twenty years old, alone in the Scottish Highlands, armed with a notebook, a pen and a flip phone. My rational brain knew it must be something large like a deer, sharpening the air with a fierce cry to ward off predators from her precious dappled baby, but at the sound of it, my head had raced with ancient gods, faerie realms and monsters long forgotten. It brought to mind Angela Carter's Erl-King, the woodland spirit-man who cares for the creatures of the land but who could do you 'grievous harm'.

All these years later, I watch the deer in my garden with my hand over my chest. He is so exposed, careless in his youth, with no mother to watch over his first solo summer. My heart aches for him and for me; it is time for me, just like the unseen deer mothers, to finally let go.

The deer fades secretly into the tangle of brambles and into the scrub as if crossing a ripple of consciousness.

Please let this mean something, I want to beg the darkening sky.

Please.

But I do not trust myself to hope any more. The symbols are not leading me to another child – a fawn of my very own – maybe only showing me glimpses of the world's constant interplays of life and death, of renewal and demise.

The symbols are showing me life goes on – and so must I.

Chapter Eleven

Cat

4th December 2023
I am lying on yet another reclining hospital bed. More cold jelly on my stomach.

This is the last time I will see her alive, swimming and kicking with those strong, spindly legs on the ultrasound monitor.

Stop kicking. Please *stop kicking*, I plead with my bump inside my mind. The more she kicks, the harder the next stage is going to be.

It is already the hardest thing I will ever have to go through.

All throughout the pregnancy, Sky has been in an awkward position, something not helped by my anteverted uterus. It had been difficult for the doctors to get a read on her head measurements, her spine, her heart, her arms. Whatever they needed to see, she wasn't going to show it.

Catch me if you can! she giggled inside me.

But today she is in exactly the right position for what needs to happen.

The doctor is tall, stylish, blonde and unsmiling. I trust her implicitly even though I know the procedure she is about to perform will change my life forever.

We are terminating Sky for medical reasons. Terminating. Bringing to a close. Ending her life. Could there be any colder way to describe what we are actually doing? We could not bring a baby this sick into the world, knowing she would be in constant pain due to her abnormalities; knowing that she would have no quality of life whatsoever; would never speak or understand us; would likely not survive more than a few minutes. We have taken the only route that was realistically available to us.

Knowing this does not stop the pain in my heart.

Of course, for many reasons, not everyone in our position would make the same decision. TFMR generally follows a diagnosis during pregnancy of congenital anomalies involving severe structural and/or functional abnormalities. In 2022, there were 3,644 pregnancies terminated for medical reasons in England, Wales and Scotland.[20] In the UK, over 70 per cent of congenital anomalies of varying severity are detected during pregnancy and, of those, around 37 per cent will result in TFMR.[21] In cases where a child is developing with conditions such as anencephaly, bilateral renal agenesis or a severe chromosomal condition like Sky, the child will almost always be stillborn or die very shortly after birth.

In a few short minutes, Sky will be administered a KCL injection – a lethal potassium shot – straight to the heart. Her death will be instant. She will feel nothing. Afterwards, I am told I will then be left in this room with Will for thirty minutes. After the time is up, another doctor will come in and double-check for signs of life on the ultrasound in case she dodged the needle and just fell asleep. I will then receive a pill that will start the first part of the induction process. Then we can go home and I will hold my dead baby inside me for another twenty-four hours. In most cases, the mother or birthing parent will be required to stay at home for forty-eight hours after the procedure but, due to my obvious distress, I am being granted a small leniency. Tomorrow evening, I will be fully induced, go into labour and give birth.

I don't think many people are aware of this – I most certainly wasn't. They think a termination is a quiet thing done under anaesthesia. When we first received the diagnosis, I thought I would awaken from a deep sleep with a deflating stomach and no signs of the little life that was once inside me – the room around me sterile and empty.

But this is not the case.

I am fully awake. And soon I will have to push.

This is what happens when a termination is administered after sixteen weeks' gestation or when a baby dies naturally in the womb after this length of time. I have been told not to move quickly when I get home, as this might make her dead body swish around inside me and cause distressing movement. I am glad I have been warned of this. Every little thing that comes out of the doctor's mouth about the procedure and what will follow is a horror story and I let each word seep into my mind like gore through cheesecloth.

Why am I having to make these decisions? I cannot believe this is happening to me.

Me. Jenn. The woman who squeals when there's a goldfinch in the garden. The girl who played with Barbie dolls in secret until she was thirteen. The child who gave her diary a pet name.

We watch the needle being assembled next to my bare and prepped belly. Tears are flowing down both sides of my face into my hair and ears but I'm trying not to make a sound so as not to cause an echo in the cavernous room. They turn off the monitors at my request, angle the computer screen away so I won't have to see my baby die right before my eyes.

As the needle goes into my numb belly, I'm clutching Will's hand, staring into his eyes, silently pleading through my tears and he is reassuring me that everything will be OK. Over and over and over.

I feel the pressure of the plunger being released and then...
A sudden lightness.
A rush.
A surge upwards.
A tiny consciousness fleeing up towards the left-hand corner of the room.
I gasp.
'I felt her go!' I grab Will's arm with both hands, pulling him closer. 'I felt her leave. She's gone.'
I am twenty-one grams lighter and she is no longer with me.

September 2024
'Good morning, baby!'
I receive a crispy 'mow' in response.
No, I'm not cooing over Linnet for once. I'm committing cat adultery. Thomas the black farm cat with his white throat and rumbling purr comes croaking over to me across the yard.
Aside from Linnet, Thomas is the furry light of my life.
Vicky, the bereavement midwife, has told me to go outside and do something fun today. Believe it or not, I do remember

what that feels like, mostly. I've been going out, seeing my friends, having little brunches in Manchester under walls of potted plants and macrame while the *Twilight* soundtrack plays in the background like we're back in 2008. Sometimes I wear a cute shade of lipstick and sometimes I buy weird lamps just because I can. But it is a different kind of fun than the pull of the summer countryside.

Being outside in the sunshine is an incomparable lightness. This year, the end of summer glows through Mother Alder's wood, dappling my arms with the pale imprints of the season's element – Fire. The bluebells are long passed and the paths have become virtually unnavigable through hard eruptions of bramble vines and the last vestiges of goosegrass tangling your feet. But if you go equipped with scissors and a hardy pair of walking trousers, you might just escape the woods alive. Under the canopy is a cool reprieve of tessellating light and shade as you wend your way through the backways of the countryside.

I rush straight to find Thomas – one of the most constant joys in my life.

At one murky point in very recent history, I had never thought of myself as a cat person. Having been torn to shreds by a friend's kittens as a teenager, I'd said a firm 'no, thank you' to any relationship with future felines. But marrying a cat person will open your eyes.

Will had grown up on a farm in rural Germany in the 1990s (think Steiner school, no TV and out on his bike in the woods from dawn until dusk – and I thought *I* had a nature-filled childhood) with around fifteen barn cats on hand at any one time. Will's favourite was the dinky tabby cat Lily, who took the journey to England with the family when they moved to Devon in the mid-2000s. I had the pleasure of meeting this darling old lady when she was around twenty years old and often sneezed on the walls and furniture, leaving trails of stringy goop in her wake. Lily was, however, an absolute sweetheart who anyone would be happy to clean up after. Whenever there was a cat at a party or on the street, Will would take the time to crouch down and stroke it. This calm cat-whisperer knew exactly what to do when the time for getting our own cat came around.

Linnet came into our lives in 2017 and – bam – I became a hardened cat lady.

Thomas is already wending around my ankles, the brown amongst his fur giving him an amber aura as the sun hits him. A true angel. He headbutts me with a force like a small tornado and I immediately oblige him by showering him in strokes and bum scratches. Thomas kneads the concrete below him, looking like he's landed in the lap of luxury, before flopping onto his back. That tummy could single-handedly heal my mental health.

'Mowww,' says Thomas, reaching up with grey-clawed paws to bring my hand back to him.

But there's something more to my obsession than just kitty cuteness, if you can believe it. Whenever I come out to the fields, I never see Thomas when I'm feeling like myself. Isn't it strange that this half-feral barn cat comes out to drool in my outstretched hand whenever I am sad?

How does he know?

Countless websites remind me that *of course* animals know when you're sad, just as humans can pick up on the subtle energy changes around them and downcast facial expressions. But from twenty streets away? Surely not.

'Spoiling him again, are yer?' the farmer calls from the barn and I grin like a child caught sneaking scraps to a puppy under the table.

'I love him!' I call back, a hint of romance in my voice. Thomas can pass my front door any day.

In many cultures, one of the first superstitions we learn is that a cat crossing your path is a warning or an uneasy type of message, taken as a sign of bad luck. They've had a bad rap since all that witch stuff happened a few hundred years ago, but probably before that too. In the ancient highlands of Scotland, a terrifying beast roamed under a cover of darkness. This large black cat with – much like little Thomas – a white spot on its chest was said to have eyes as large as saucers, with an eerie green glow. Its fur stood on end as it spat its displeasure at anyone who should be unlucky enough to cross it in the mountains, leaping from the crags. Not only was the Cat Sith (pronounced 'cat shee') a fairy and a shapeshifter, legend says that the Cat Sith was once a witch who could turn into a cat nine times in her life and predict the deaths of people for the year ahead. But it was more than her foresight that was feared.

During the Celtic festival of Samhain (or modern-day Halloween), the Cat Sith would lurk in the streets and the funeral parlours looking for souls to feed on. When the people realised that their dead loved ones were being preyed upon, they would fiercely guard their recently deceased bodies, keeping the room as cold as could be to deter the warmth-loving cat. Although the locals tried to appease it with saucers of milk and other offerings or scare it away by lighting bonfires and wearing masks, the Cat Sith would still loiter in the shadows, waiting to dart forth and curse the home of anyone who had been foolish enough not to protect themselves.

Want to let your cat outside on Samhain? Scottish villagers might advise against it, believing the Cat Sith might possess a living cat to carry out its dark deeds. Samhain isn't too far off and I will definitely be keeping Linnet inside on such a potent night.

However, in modern Britain, black cats are often seen as having the opposite connotations. If a black cat crosses your path in Luton, you're about to get a sprinkling of good luck, and it is even thought that if you're a woman who receives a black cat as a gift, you're destined to have a happy marriage. Sailors believed that keeping a black cat on board would protect them from storms and shipwrecks, and fishermen's wives often kept black cats at home to ensure their husbands' safe return from sea. Lucky little blighters... but talk about mixed messages.

We've come a long way from believing cats to be the Devil's right hand. In the media during the 1960s, Morticia Addams' favoured pet, Kitty Kat – a ferocious-looking mountain lion – is doted on by the family and produces eruptions of laughter from a hysterical studio audience. Samantha's Siamese cat Zip Zip in *Bewitched* is given the same treatment. From this point on, cats started to become comic side characters – harmless, docile and just there for the aww factor. In Jill Murphy's 1974 books series *The Worst Witch*, main character Mildred Hubble adores her cat, Tabby, who keeps getting into mischief and is described as a little bit 'hopeless'; *Sabrina the Teenage Witch*'s Salem, the best-loved talking cat of 1990s TV, is a flamboyant, wise-cracking comedy king; and where would Harry Potter be without the dry wit of shapeshifting Professor McGonagall?

People's opinions on cats flip-flop back and forth depending on the century in a strange love-hate cycle. But I know Thomas is just a little sweetheart with a penchant for bum scratches. Nothing magical here.

Besides, I'm not supposed to be thinking about the signs, am I? I suppose I'm on some kind of Pagan hiatus. Cold, hard facts only. Subscribe me to the *Guardian*, please, and let's forget everything I've believed for the past twenty-one years of my life. I'm not sure it's as simple as that but removing the added pressure of symbol-spotting from my daily walks has definitely improved my mood and allowed me to notice the seasons more than my grey and bleary mind had managed recently.

I arrive at home, uplifted and radiant from my Thomas encounter, and immediately feel guilty as Linnet sniffs my hand (very thoroughly) at the door. 'Traitor,' she spits with her eyes.

I contort my face into an admission of guilt to the wild thing inside my house.

Oh, I do adore cats.

Especially because Linnet had been basically feral up until two years ago. We had adopted her from the local shelter back in 2017 when she was two years old and had been told she was an indoor cat, which at the time was perfect because we lived in a second-floor flat just outside of Manchester city centre. But it soon became apparent that Linnet did not like this living arrangement and basically hated us with all her might.

Now, seven years and a move to the suburbs later, she is a changed woman. I haven't managed to keep her on my lap longer than fifteen minutes but I'm working on it.

Why won't you just let me mother you, Linnet?

I often think about Linnet's family, where she came from, and whom she inherited her nastiest traits from. 'Why are you such a bitch, Linnet?' we often asked, hands throbbing with scratches. I settle down on the couch and pat the cushion beside me. Linnet hops up and assumes a loaf position and I let my fingers trail over her nose and forehead, once, twice, twenty times, and the purr appears, vibrating the cushion below her like a miniature vehicle of healing.

I'd heard of instances of female cats and other animals adopting the young of their species in times of desperate need and wondered if Linnet had secretly adopted me instead.

My blindsiding grief journey has been transformative in more ways than one. And I have given it my all:

- witchcraft healing rituals
- Reiki
- reading about grief, trauma and baby loss
- support groups
- traditional Chinese Medicine
- fertility reflexology
- Stoic philosophy
- journalling
- gratitude journalling
- shamanic journeying
- somatic yoga
- long hikes in nature
- screaming into my pillow

You name it, I've probably tried it on my quest for healing. But nothing has worked so much as the constant love and gentle purrs of my Linnet Cat.

However, I'm ready to try one final thing.

I bite the inside of my lip as I sit down in Lucy's office.

'Wow, you've brought a whole lot of people with you today,' she says, looking mildly exasperated.

'Oh, I'm sorry!' I say, as I look around the empty room.

'It's not your fault,' she laughs. 'There are just a lot of people who are looking after you.'

Lucy and I have known each other for several years since I became one of her Reiki clients but she is more well known locally and internationally as a psychic medium. In many of our Reiki sessions, I've seen shadows flickering in the corner of the room and watched them with wide eyes as the music cut out and wouldn't start again. When I had just entered my second trimester in 2023, I went to Lucy for Reiki and before I sat down, she said, 'Fourteen weeks.' I blinked back at her, wondering which spirit had chosen to do my pregnancy reveal for me. Even though I'd been reaching out to trees and magical creatures for over half my life, I hadn't quite got the hang of nattering with the spirits – but around Lucy, they never stopped talking.

Lucy's bright blue eyes pierce mine from under her sleek dark hair (she probably hears 'You're Sherilyn Fenn's double!' on the daily, although I've yet to say the words to her) with a sharpness that always makes me sit up straight. I often feel like my skin is made of glass around her as her gaze misses nothing.

So, I'm here today to ask some questions.

It's been a very long time since I've allowed myself anywhere near predictions of the future, having put my Tarot cards to bed a while ago. Every spiritual slap on the wrist telling me to be patient and to learn my lessons felt like a punch to the gut, but at this point, nine months later, I'm ready for some divine advice.

Whatever it might be.

We sit opposite each other in the small, bright, crystal-loaded room that seems to vibrate with energy. I don't know what I'm expecting – perhaps dimmed lights and strange voices – but the Big Light stays firmly on and Lucy launches straight in.

'Your grandma just told me to put my Tarot cards away. Feisty woman, was she, your grandma?'

I laugh. My very Christian grandma certainly knew her own mind! Relief floods over me as I think of my little white-haired grandma in her purple special-occasion cardigan and gold bracelet, waving at me from the corner of the room. I miss her with a fierceness that draws my heart upwards to the edge of my chest.

'OK, so your grandad is here too but Grandma isn't letting him speak. She's showing me cherry Madeira cake and, oh, did she have a slow decline over six months?' Lucy holds her chest.

I press my lips together and nod, remembering that very unhappy time in 2021 where Grandma's heart slowly gave out.

Lucy nods back. 'She wants you to know that she was very ready to go. She's also giving me excruciating headaches. Was that something to do with her passing?'

I frown. 'No, there were no headaches that we were aware of.'

'Oh!' says Lucy, eyes wide. 'You're the one with the headaches, it's you!'

'Well!' I laugh. 'I am, I've been having trouble with my eyes recently and my new glasses are giving me bad headaches.'

'Your grandma is saying you really need to get that sorted out. Can you tell her to stop trying to show me now? We've figured it out. Ow.'

Lucy then gives me an incredibly accurate description of my grandma's personality – down to her Stoic nature and her collector's eye – and relates some relationship advice from beyond the grave. 'There are other people trying to talk but she's not letting them!' Grandma certainly has a lot to tell me today and I couldn't be more grateful to hear her straight-talking ways channelled through Lucy.

As the session continues, I'm scribbling down every word Grandma tells me when I remember why I'm actually here today.

'Is Sky with her?' I ask.

'Yes, Sky is with her.'

I grip the sides of my seat.

Sky. Hi, baby.

'Can I speak with her?'

Lucy nods. 'Your grandma just keeps showing me this beautiful little girl and telling me how beautiful she is. She is so proud of you.'

'Thank you, Grandma!' I say, wiping a tear away. I'm looking into the empty corner of the room where Lucy's gaze sometimes travels. What a wonder it must be to have this gift, although I know that if I possessed it, I might have allowed myself to be driven even madder over the past year.

'Now,' Lucy continues, 'with such little babies, we can still communicate with them but we might not get much, do you understand?'

I nod ferociously, willing to try.

Lucy's eyes trail off into the distance. 'She's showing me lips. Do you know why that might be?'

I think back to all the kisses I planted so gently on her cool forehead and cheeks in those brief moments we had had together. I'm so happy that she is remembering me this way.

'She's telling me that she really loves her name. And have you got it engraved on a plant somewhere? She's showing me flowers.'

I smile and realise she means the Sky Garden, fully in bloom and trailing forget-me-nots and campion over the sides of its bright blue pots.

I wish I'd written a list of questions but I had no idea this was how a mediumship reading works. I thought I was going to get whatever information I was given, not have the opportunity to interview my grandma and my dead child. My mind is reeling.

'Does Sky know that we love her?'

'Absolutely, yes. She knows it deeply.'

Good. Good. Good. Good.

'Can I ask... will I see her again?'

Lucy looks me dead in the eye and says, 'Yes, you definitely will.'

I pause and think about what I've just asked.

'Do you mean after I pass over or do you mean that she'll come back to us as another child?'

Her gaze clarifies further. 'She is coming back to you, Jenn. You will see her again in this life.'

A baby. A new baby.

I find myself nodding as if my life depends on it. I understand. I'm here looking for answers. I understand.

But do I believe it? I turn my eye inward as if I am about to access a trance state but instead tune in to my intuition.

The fact of the matter is, I know I am meant to be a mother. No, it didn't work out this first or second time around but I know that I have so much love to give that when a baby does finally make its way to my arms – through IVF, adoption or a natural conception – the love will rise up from the swell of my chest to create a mural of light and laughter and the textures of our life together. That love will be like no other.

I believe with all my heart what Lucy is telling me.

In this room, all the answers are at my fingertips but I feel like I am not quite ready to know when that child may come. The ups and downs of this year have been almost too much for one person to bear – if I pin my hopes on another date that comes and passes, will I be able to get past that hurdle and not crumble? I still have a lot of healing to do and have already found out so much from beyond the veil today. I have more questions: does communicating with the living tire the spirits out? I wouldn't want to drain her energy in any way. Is she around me often, even though I can't feel her? But to know she is coming back to me is so much more than I could ever have hoped to know.

It has been a long nine months but I hope she knows that I would wait forever if it meant that I was going to meet her again alive.

Instead of dissolving into tears, I take a deep breath and say, 'Thank you, Grandma, for taking care of her for us. I love you very much.'

I am so glad I came here today.

On the way home, I take the path through a sun-bright meadow bordered by scrubby reeds, the remnants of a lost bog where reed buntings and bitterns may once have nested. Now, the meadow is home to the occasional Highland cow, which always makes me judder to a stop and marvel, but there are also the sedge warblers, reed warblers and a panoply of comma butterflies. Its arid, dusty mud track is often so waterlogged in the autumn and winter that someone has placed an impromptu boardwalk made of a cut-up old wardrobe next to it for the nervous traveller. This land is so out of keeping with an area concentrated with moorland habitat so it feels like a small oasis close to the train tracks and I am thrilled to have it for as long as the developers can turn a blind eye.

I'm trying to determine whether the call I hear is a sedge or reed warbler – listening out for the flutey notes that define the sedge's song – when a single magpie THWACKS down on the path ahead of me. It rocks forward on its scaly legs, its overlong tail standing erect for a second like the caricature of a wren. Its black eyes gleam in the afternoon sun.

In my mind's eye, I see the flickering quartz of Newgrange and the corvid with its beak upturned towards the sky.

But I take a deep breath. I plant my trainers into the dust track.

Sky is coming back to me. Maybe not this month or the next, but I have a renewed belief in the link between my life and hers. So what if the signs have been leading me on a wild goose chase these past several months? I have to trust in what I feel deep in my stomach, that I will have a healthy baby one day.

I keep my chin high as I walk down that path to as close as the magpie will let me. It caterwauls away across the meadow, disturbing crickets and stonechats, commas and sedge warblers, but I keep on walking straight ahead.

When I get home later, Will looks knackered from another long day and I wring my hands. I have so much new knowledge that is ready to fall out of my lips but is there much use in telling him? My loving, non-spiritual husband? While he may not understand the full depth of my feelings, Will has had a tough year too and it shows in his face, even if he can't let it all out in so many words. I wonder how I look to him.

When processing grief, everyone is different and I have come to understand just how different the situation looks to the father of a stillborn child, to someone who does not have to live with the bodily trauma of the loss every single second of their day. I think about how I might be if I too could compartmentalise what had happened but I realise I never could because she lived inside me and part of her always will. Our experiences of Sky are different – as much as that is difficult for me to digest. While it is not the same for Will, he has been suffering in his own way and he could do with some hope too.

I give him a cup of tea and decide to test the waters.

'I went to see Lucy today.'

'Oh yeah?'

'I spoke to Sky.'

Will lifts his head to me, waiting. I notice his blue eyes are a little wider than normal.

I tell him everything I've just heard.

Afterwards, we sit in silence while Linnet comes in to lie next to us on the rug so that we form a small triangle of tanned skin and burnished fur – a real little coven. Our otherworldly messenger blinks her soft green eyes gently up past our faces and into the top corner of the room.

Will nods, processing everything I've said. 'She'll come back to us soon,' he says with a small smile, edged firmly with hope.

I squeeze his hand. 'She'll be here.'

We are a simple three, just waiting with a deep knowing for our fourth and tiniest member to finally arrive.

Chapter Twelve

Crow

The moment the midwife put her in my arms, I knew that I would never be the same again.

I took in her ruddy little limbs, her scrunched-up face, the strong nose and the tiny six-toed feet with such joy. Not sadness – joy. Happiness for finally seeing her after all those long months since we had first started trying to imagine her into the world. I knew her little mouselike soul was no longer inside her body – I had felt it go – but maybe the essence of her was in the room, hovering somewhere above my middle. Maybe she was there shouting a rallying cry that came through as pinpoints of otherworldly light, or maybe she was there just wanting to see the look on my face as I finally beheld hers. I whimpered as I laboured, I didn't scream. My body had not wanted to let go of the precious weight of her but after nine hours of contractions, she was birthed in three pushes – too small for full dilation to be necessary. After the second push, I had turned to Will, my eyes wild, and said, 'She's coming.'

And then she was here. And not really here at all.

During the difficult pregnancy, when I had become too anaemic to leave my house, it had been all too easy to place the blame on the fragile body growing inside me. There were times when I despised being pregnant, truly, truly hated it, and wished her gone. All throughout those five and a half months, I had boggled at how little we are taught about this huge life event; how the 'morning sickness' can be completely debilitating so that you can't get out of bed, nevermind focus on work or even look after yourself; how you can't eat anything for months without being sick; how the hormones don't just cause postpartum depression but an everyday sort of depression that tints everything in greige. I was outraged, affronted and would complain loudly about it with my pregnant friends and other mothers. We'd rip into a pack of ginger biscuits together and berate the patriarchy that kept 'women's issues' safely underfunded and tucked out of the way, uncontrollable bile rising up our throats.

Wasn't this supposed to be a sacred time? Wasn't I supposed to rub my bare belly in a sunlit garden and telepathically send her love notes? Shouldn't I have told her I loved her every day since July?

In *Matrescence* Lucy Jones says: 'From the moment I was pregnant, I didn't just feel different. I was different. I am different. On a cellular level. I would never be singular again.' But I had fought that feeling, I had resisted the physical and hormonal changes in me, begging for my previous iteration – the Maiden, not the Mother – to re-encircle me and re-gift me with her unknowingness.

But Jones is right. Once you have had a baby grow inside you, you are never the same.

The pregnancy had completely altered me forever to give me my newly widened hips and my thick, lustrous hair. My baby had changed me from the inside out. But that's not all.

During pregnancy, a phenomenon occurs called foetal microchimerism. This is where a baby's cells migrate into its mother through the umbilical cord and remain in her body for years, layering themselves into various tissues such as the brain, thyroid and the breasts, although likely other areas as well. These cells, which are often stem cells, can transform into different tissue types depending on where they lodge. While some cells are cleared out by the mother's immune system, others persist, potentially altering the mother's health – for better or worse. Body temperature, milk quality, cancer – all of these things can be influenced by the baby's cells and their subtle tweaks to the mother's body, with studies showing that these cells can migrate to future children, tangling themselves into a living, breathing family tree.

I wondered what Sky had left behind inside me. Had any of her cells crossed the pulsing red boundary into my body to freewheel themselves into my corners and bends? What might she pass to her siblings – the misty-faced children of my future – whenever they decided to arrive?

While my information on her would always be limited, I knew a lot about her resilience. Against all odds, she had held on for five and a half months – maybe she would have lasted longer if we hadn't made that final and fatal decision for her. In spite of her condition and all the abnormalities that she faced, she had kept going. Fighting to live and fighting to maybe meet me one day.

If I were half as resilient and loving as she was, then I knew I would be OK in the end.

It was only when I saw her that I truly understood what it had all been about. A new and roaring cascade of love hit the world's edges, pouring straight from my heart and aimed at her lifeless body. The love was almost unbearable, numbing my physical self so that I saw only her and nothing else, as if she were made of light itself and was all I ever needed to sustain me.

This was what I had been put on this earth to feel.

As I sat with her in the crook of my left arm, I knew my role in the world had changed irrevocably. There was no going back now. I was her mother and I would love her fiercely for as long as her soul would have me.

31st October 2024

A popping noise starts low on the horizon and I stop in my tracks, turning my head towards the sound.

In the lilac-threaded autumn sky, crows are following the ridges of the clouds westward to their evening roost. They come in waves: the first smattering arriving quietly and then the second wave – bigger and more boisterous than the last – creating a sea edged in black foam. They barely seem to flap, soaring like woodcut carvings, wings outstretched, catching the currents that I can't even imagine down here on the cobbled country road.

I follow them across the sky, craning my neck, chin stuck up like a signal flag. From down here, it is impossible to tell which are the young and which are the adults.

The sun is falling behind the Pennine hills, with the crows forming an arc of darkness, as if they are the night themselves chasing the daylight. But really they are only going home to hunch their shoulders and release their taut wings for the evening after a long day in the air. I wonder which mighty tree carries this many crows – the murder making its branches heavy, loose black feathers collecting in its root furrows.

Despite the date and my troubled history with animal symbolism, the birds no longer fill me with fear. I take note of their warnings and let them go, knowing the story is much bigger than them. They flash up their warnings for this second, this moment, but my path is longer and wider than they can illuminate. The crows and I are companion creatures: they carry the weight of their symbolism wherever they go and I carry my story under the folds of my wings, ready to fly forward and continue my story.

Today is Samhain, the festival with a name that translates to 'summer's end'. It is both the start and endpoint of the Witch's Year. As with Beltane, the veil between the worlds of the living and the dead is whisper thin, meaning it is easy for spirits to cross over the divide. Today, the dead walk amongst us, and it is also easier for us to make that crossing in our astral bodies to seek out arcane knowledge for ourselves. Divination is a large part of the festival of Samhain. The Crone goddess Cerridwen stirs her cauldron, revealing messages in its steam, and flickers of wisdom are shuffled fiercely from Tarot decks. The answers are there for us to find, if we lift the folds of night just so.

The crows soar noisily away from me and I blink as if I'm emerging from the dark wood surrounding their roost. Over in the west, the light left in their wake has reached a fever pitch of violent pinks and lurid purples. This is my favourite spot to come and watch the sky dance; no, I never did see the aurora but this is a close second. It's in places like this, looking out over the rolling moor-topped Lancashire hills, that you can really feel the weight of the sky; how its many sunset colours add thick acrylic paint to the inverted canvas; how they roll together in dense wheels of gold and coral and vermilion, merging when touched by the heavy water droplets of a cloud.

A greenish pallor tinges the horizon and I realise I have maybe twenty minutes to get home before twilight falls and the ghosts come out.

Sorry, trick or treaters, tonight I'm going into full ritual mode.

At home, I let Linnet outside while I cleanse the house, fumigating the living room with a thick stick of garden sage that sends plumes of grey smoke up my white walls. I'm hoping the Cat Sith isn't lurking but I feel like Lin will be safe overseen by the Earth Spirits that reside in our garden.

I fan the smoke over my Samhain Pagan altar that I have created on the living room coffee table to remove any lingering energies. It is overflowing with pictures of my grandparents as well as objects they held dear. I wind a golden locket through the candles that Grandma had given me on my confirmation day back in 2001. There is a small wooden duck they brought back from a trip to Oregon, a tiny golden ring they bought for me when I was a child that still fits my pinkie finger, and the porcelain Green Lady who once presided over many family meals and birthday buffets in the dining room. But there are also tributes to Sky there. While she is not one of my ancestors – rather a descendant – I have hopes that my grandma is holding her in that sunlit kitchen with the smell of radiator dust and fresh ironing hanging in the air around them. Her ashes stand on the right of the altar, a locket containing the fine dust of her in the centre and the woollen heart from her memory box to the left.

It feels complete. Grandparents and great-grandchild held in one place.

Linnet gives a sudden, sharp MEOW outside the back door and I rush – with a mother's urgency – to open it for her.

'Lin?'

But she isn't there. She is up on the half-wall that divides our garden from the bins. Her tail is a burst of fur and she looks at me with wide green eyes.

'What is it, baby? What have you seen?'

The Cat Sith really is in my garden?

In answer, she stares at the back fence that borders the playing field. I freeze when I see the long, dead willowherb stems swaying violently behind the fenceposts, illuminated in our garden's automatic floodlight. There is something on the other side of my fence. It is moving and it is big.

What is it? A dog? Has the deer come back? Or is it human?

I turn on my heel and run upstairs, intent on getting a look over the fence to see what local ruffian has been spying on my house. I fling the bathroom window open and watch the shuddering plants. 'What are you?' I mutter.

But then my heart jolts into my throat and I let out a throttled gasp as an adult red fox – which looks almost the size of me – bounds out from behind the conservatory and scrabbles over the back fence to join its mate. Its speed and sheer size have me reaching for my throat.

The pair ricochets away into the scrub, bending saplings and branches as they escape. A torrent of crows comes down after them from a nearby tree, their crackles filling the air. It's like I'm watching all the Celtic myths I have researched over the past year spilling from a portal in my garden, blending the cry of the mournful curlew with the bounding fertility of the young, virile stag. The lush curve of the fox's tail momentarily curves around the full-bodied notes of a rook's warning. My garden has never felt so wild and filled with magic. On Samhain, no less!

The pair of foxes has startled me into remembrance. I know their message. It is one of fighting for survival.

And survive I have, despite the world's most brutal challenges.

While I am resolved to see past and around the symbols of the world, this is a message that I can feel vibrating deep within me – I will survive and I will continue to heal.

I go back inside, rattled and thrumming with stirrings of power.

On my altar, I place a plate of soul cakes – a traditional Samhain currant cake that I baked the night before as an edible ancestor offering. The plate contains five soul cakes – four large ones for my grandparents and a smaller baby-sized one for Sky made from an offcut of dough. I cast a ritual circle of protection around me and call in the Four Elements – Earth, Air, Fire and Water – as well as the goddess of the darkest parts of the year.

It is time for my Samhain ritual to begin.

'Cerridwen, I welcome you into my circle. Bless this space with your power and keep me safe as I speak with my ancestors. I invoke thee, I invoke thee, I invoke thee. Hail and welcome.'

I wait for a few moments as I press my senses out into the air, waiting for the Welsh goddess Cerridwen to fill the space with her presence.

She does not disappoint.

Within the modern form of Paganism, Cerridwen is viewed as a vital part of the Triple Goddess, rounding off the triad of Maiden, Mother and Crone. She might have long white hair, a wizened brow and a walking cane, but she is certainly *no* fluffy grandma.

Cerridwen is the overseer of the colder months of the year – forcing the chill in the air so that we stay indoors on those blacker-than-black nights and turn inwards to reflect on our experiences of the past year. She is the ruler of transformation, creativity and inspiration, processes that germinate from the darkest of places. In Celtic mythology, Cerridwen is a goddess of the underworld, swirling her cauldron of hidden knowledge from this world and the next. Her cauldron holds the mysteries of life, death and rebirth – the ultimate transformation.

And transform I have.

Under a cover of the goddess's darkness, I begin my ancestor ritual:

'This is the night when the gateway between
our world and the spirit world is thinnest.
Tonight is a night to call out to those who came before us.
Tonight we honour our ancestors.'

In the stillness, a weight settles around me. The goddess? My grandparents? Sky? I don't know. But I am willing to sit with them and take stock of life's truths.

'Spirits of our ancestors, I call to you,
and I welcome you to join me for this night.
Beryl, Bill, Frances, Ken, Sky,
I know you watch over me always,
protecting me and guiding me,
and, tonight, I thank you.
I invite you to join me and share in this feast.'
I gesture to the plate of soul cakes.

'On this night of Samhain, send me your strength and protection, guide me as I head into my uncertain future and share with me the knowledge that will keep me on my path.'

I sit and breathe in. The air is thick with spirits and ripe with knowledge.

Over the course of a single year, I realise I have learned many things:

1. Life is so fragile and deeply precious. We need to treat it with so much respect for just being able to *exist* in this not-so-nurturing world. Knowing this has allowed me the chance to reevaluate my attitudes towards all living things; it has ultimately brought me closer to my spirituality – in the most roundabout of ways – and connected me more intensely with the living world around me. We only have to look around us, at any deep-furrowed willow tree or fresh, crisp daffodil, to find the beauty of this incredible, green-hearted life around us. What a miracle to be alive and to exist *here*.

2. I no longer fear death. I have surrounded myself with stories of the Otherworld, near-death experiences and about what happens when we die (my house has been a morbid curiosity shop, can you tell?). Having seen and read dozens of first-hand accounts while trying to convince myself that

my baby's soul was safe and well, I feel I can say with some confidence that the soul feels no pain after death. Seemingly, we are reunited with our loved ones and feel only immense joy and lightness. Which is a much happier side to the picture than I had imagined before and one that I hold in my heart. Knowing that I will join my daughter there someday now feels like a gentle kiss on the cheek rather than the yawning darkness that I felt before.

3. The faces we present to the world are just shallow masks in the face of authentic feeling. Before all this, I spent a lot of time curating my online presence and obsessing over how I was perceived by the wider world. It consumed me far more than I would ever care to admit. The existence of social media – in its current form of usage – is a way to showcase to the world the array of possessions we have that make us unique, that allow our personalities to be displayed through the money we spend. The futility of trying to carve out uniqueness and skew how I am perceived in this space somehow seems silly to me now and I want to spend my time on other pursuits. It has been an ego death for me, that's for sure. Social media and the other crutches we use to present a false face to the world can afford to be chopped from our lives. What is it that you really want to do with your life? What will make you feel like you've had a life well-lived? These feel like the real questions I want to dedicate my time to now.

4. Humans really do have the capability to overcome anything. However, we have to find the drive to heal within ourselves. Throughout my years of poor mental health, depression and anxiety, I would never have imagined that I could get through something as huge and life-changing as this and still be *living*. I am just one person, but I feel like this

whole experience has been a testament to humanity's drive to survive. I, perhaps more than anyone, am shocked at the animal drive to persist in the face of horrors; our resilience knows no bounds. We have the capacity to heal and to get through the most challenging of times, but this has to come from a desire to grow and a wanting to meet new versions of ourselves along the way. We are stronger than we could ever know.

5. Good things do not always come to the good. This has perhaps been my hardest lesson of all.

Even in our 'enlightened' and learned age, science and medicine do not save the day 100 per cent of the time and they still cannot explain the process of death outside of the cellular. Sometimes the mystery of it all persists and perhaps I will never have the answers I seek. This large offering tray of life experience has made me question my views and my values and changed my perception of where I sit in the Universe's game. I do one day hope to know why this happened and if there was some greater meaning to being dealt a Sympathy Hand. But I will have to be content with not knowing and just accepting – for now.

This book is, without a doubt, the hardest thing I have ever written. Confronting the trauma of the past year and seeing the stark facts written out in magpie colours has meant reliving the horror with every edit. But I continued to write with the purpose of this resonating with someone else's experience. If this book helps someone other than myself to explore their own grief or find their strength in the face of the most terrible event a parent could go through, then I know it will all have meant something. This is a huge comfort to me. I am grateful beyond measure or words that I have been surrounded by the most supportive family and friends known to humankind. The kindness, gentleness and strength of those around me have been, perhaps, the secret sixth lesson I have learned from grief.

But that is where I want to leave this book.

There are two things I hope people can take from my writing.

Firstly, 'everything happens for a reason' is absolute bullshit – if you see the reason as a punishment. But I have found another reason amongst the chaos. I want you to know that if you lose your baby, it is not some higher power's way of punishing you. It is absolutely shit. And it is probably the worst thing that will ever happen to you. No one deserves it. But I have carved out a journey that has ultimately helped me to start healing my mind and my spirit, to become a stronger version of myself. Before Sky, I did not know I could become stronger or that this strength would help me to understand myself better, and perhaps that was the reason behind it all. I did not know the full capacity and depth of the love I can feel, and I am so much stronger than I could ever have believed possible. Yes, there are days when my loss feels as hollow and stripped of colour as it did on that very first night home from the hospital. But those days are few and far between now and, when they happen, I can pull myself out of them quicker than I could before. Much of what they tell you about grief is false. As I've said, those five stages are not the same for everyone. But that last stage – acceptance – might just be true.

Time heals. Nature heals. And this is to whom they have both led me: myself.

The second thing is this: little by little, in barely perceptible increments, things do get better. I didn't believe it either in those first few months but now, over ten months later, I can find the beauty in things again. I have hope for the future. But, goddess, do I miss her. That never changes.

I have spoken openly about my experiences on almost every platform where I have a voice and have received so many other stories like mine that wanted desperately to be heard. If there was an ultimate reason for this disaster to happen to me, I only wish it was so that some goodness could come out of it. Like so many other mothers, I did not get to hear my baby cry or gurgle or laugh, but I hope that by writing this I can provide some comfort, relief or companionship to others on those dark nights of the soul.

I have written what I know of mine and Sky's story so far and I have hope that she will come back to me one day. Ten months on, I appreciate that I am still very fresh on my journey. I wonder what I may be like in five years' time when I have fully grown around my grief like a Mother Alder absorbing a close-growing sapling. Will I have any seedlings of my own? I do not yet have that knowledge for sure. No, there is no new baby. Not yet, anyway. This is a solemn reality I have to face every day and the nursery is getting rather dusty these days. I have not given up hope that the tiny babygrows in the top drawer will one day be worn, but right now, I can focus on the small things. I can see a friend's baby and not crumple inside. I can keep my breath measured and walk through the sunset fields. I can sit in the garden with Linnet and a cup of tea and allow myself to listen to the birdsong.

In the first few months after my baby's death and birth, I told a dear friend of mine that losing Sky had changed me as a person forever. And she said to me: 'I am looking forward to meeting the new you.'

This is the new me and I hope she is helping others through this experience.

I sit at my Samhain altar and the candles flicker all at once despite the closed windows. The autumnal chill of the room is strong but there is a sudden, gradual warmth in my lap where my hands lie upturned. I fold my elbow into a crook where a small head could rest and close my eyes as the space fills with a soft and gentle twenty-one grams.

Sky.

As I finally hold her spirit close to my body, I realise that my healing journey wasn't to have another baby as quickly as I possibly could, to power on and replace the child I lost. It was to learn quietly about the darkness of the world, to accept it and then to learn about myself, as painful as the process has been. The months have turned on, as the Wheel of the Year famously does – it stops for no one – and I have more knowledge on this turn than the last. I do not know what is next for me, but I am trying to find peace with the unknown. I trust that what is meant for me will find me in the Universe's overall plan, even if I do wish it would hurry the hell up. But I also know that I will love this tiny baby for my whole life.

Linnet hops down from the shadows and saunters across the room, stopping at the boundary of my energetic circle, compelled by a hidden wall of luminescence. She slow-blinks at me in the candlelight and I slow-blink back.

'Do you feel her, Lin?' I whisper, a smile playing about my lips. Linnet sits, her eyes trained on me, a messenger seeing aeons and colours and breaks in the ripples of time all at once. 'Of course. I have been trying to tell you all along.'

I have finally felt Sky's spirit here with me. Where she has always been.

So I will sit here a while longer with the ghosts of my ancestors and my sweet, darling child, and keep finding renewed purpose, surrender and reasons to survive in the Samhain dark as the candle flames light up the edges of the spirits around me.

Acknowledgements

The premise of this book was originally very different. So different, in fact, that I don't recognise those old pages in the buried files of my laptop. I was partway through writing *Underwing* when we got the terrible, terrible news from the hospital. I was twenty-three weeks and three days pregnant when I gave birth to my stillborn daughter at Royal Oldham Hospital, three weeks before Christmas 2023. I thought I'd seen some things in my life, but nothing in the whole world could have prepared me for what happened over the course of those few weeks leading up to the final – devastatingly final – event.

The world was very quiet for quite some time. Which is when I decided to write about what had happened in the hopes that it might help me make sense of the hole in my world.

In the thick of my grief, I cried more tears than I ever knew it was possible for a human to cry. And then, when I started to write this book, I cried some more. I whimpered through some paragraphs. I had to close my laptop and walk away a lot. But I knew that, ultimately, I wanted to write this book.

I had several goals: 1) to share an experience that is often kept locked behind closed doors and yet is so startlingly common; 2) to give others the opening to speak about their own experiences of baby loss; 3) to express that baby loss is just as life-changing as losing a parent, partner or friend – it is not something to be swept under the carpet; and most of all 4) to honour Sky's memory. She was too young to be added to the official register, which feels so utterly wrong to me. I gave birth to her as any mother would give birth to their full-term child, yet there is no record of her presence on this earth; no file to add her name to. The idea that no one would ever know of her existence or how much she meant to us creates a physical sickness in me.

While I have tried to be as honest and real as possible in the spirit of authenticity, there are parts of this story that were just too harrowing to tell. I have not touched on the miscarriage I had at the end of summer 2024 and the extent of my symptoms during the IVF process. There is already so much trauma in these pages that I did not feel it necessary to further add to this. But I wanted to share with you that this was mindfully done and is not meant to minimise the pain and suffering of people undergoing these experiences.

I could not have got through this time without my beautiful, stoic and hopeful husband, Will. Or Linnet, the calico dreamboat that wakes me up at five a.m. every day. My friends and family, as well as the healthcare professionals and spiritual healers who surrounded us, have been incredible. Mum, Dad, Caroline Lane, Adam Hamer, Hannah Perl, Jessica Frith, Polly Frith, Lottie Blake, Charlotte Varela, Nicola Semple, Chantelle Salkeld, Lizzie Devine, Nicky Head, Alex Cracknell-Plume, Doug Brakewell, Rachel Goswell, Vicki Harrison, Kat Hamilton, Emma Roberts – you have helped me more than you could ever know. Vicky Sumner at the Saint Mary's Bereavement Midwives Team, I truly don't know what I would have done without you and your kindness. And the same goes for you, Jo Palmer: your guidance has changed my whole life.

I also want to say thank you to my exploration buddies, Laurie Cookson and Beverley Wass, and to Hannah Sanders for her incredible knowledge of witchcraft and for her kind heart. Suzanne Cooper: your help is a treasure to me. Lucy Robinson: thank you for your continued support throughout this whole process. Elaine Abraham from Finding Rainbows – you helped me later on when I didn't realise I still needed it: thank you so much. Florence: I hope you aren't too sad if you read this when you're older.

Of course, a huge, huge thank you to the wonderful Hannah MacDonald at September Publishing and my absolutely brilliant agent Charlotte Atyeo at Greyhound Literary for speaking with me honestly and openly, and for allowing me to write this from my heart.

But most of all, this book is for Sky Stobart-Lane, who never got to see her namesake and who will be loved forever.

Useful Organisations

These are some of the charities that helped me through the hardest time of my life. They offer a range of support groups, counselling, group activities, written resources and peer-to-peer advice.

Sands sands.org.uk
Petals petalscharity.org
Tommy's tommys.org
Relax with Lucy (via the Ellie's Gift app) relaxwithlucy.co.uk
TFMR Mamas tfmrmamas.com
Finding Rainbows (Manchester specific) findingrainbows.org
Still Parents (Manchester specific) whitworth.manchester.ac.uk/whats-on/exhibitions/pastexhibitions/stillparents/stillparentsproject/

Other charities

SOFT UK specialises in helping the families of those with children who have Trisomy 13 and Trisomy 18 (Patau's and Edwards' Syndrome) soft.org.uk

Further Reading

In the months following Sky's death, I wanted to find out how to heal in the most helpful and meaningful way. Here is a list of the books I read that helped me to move down the steps of the grief ladder, bringing me closer to putting my feet back on safe ground. I have also included Lucy Jones's book here as, while it does not touch on baby loss, it helped me to understand more of what had happened inside me during the time that Sky was alive.

The Body Keeps the Score by Bessel van der Kolk
When the Body Says No by Gabor Maté
The Myth of Normal by Gabor Maté
A Pocketful of Happiness by Richard E. Grant
Between Death and Life by Dolores Cannon
Grief Works by Julia Samuel
Her Birth by Rebecca Goss
Matrescence: On the Metamorphosis of Pregnancy, Childbirth and Motherhood by Lucy Jones

References

1. Elizabeth von Muggenthaler, 'The felid purr: A healing mechanism?', *The Journal of the Acoustical Society of America*, 110, 2666 (2001), https://doi.org/10.1121/1.4777098.
2. Ethel Stefana Drower, *The Mandaeans of Iraq and Iran: Their Cults, Customs, Magic, Legends, and Folklore*, The Clarendon Press, 1937.
3. Annie Worsley, *Windswept: Life, Nature and Deep Time in the Scottish Highlands*, William Collins, 2023.
4. Gabor Maté, *When the Body Says No: The Hidden Cost of Stress*, Vermilion, 2019.
5. Julia Samuel, *Grief Works: Stories of Life, Death and Surviving*, Penguin Life, 2018.
6. Dr Nicola Hemmings, 'Curlew recovery and the case of the fragile eggs', 27 July 2022, University of Sheffield, https://www.sheffield.ac.uk/biosciences/news/curlew-recovery-and-case-fragile-eggs.
7. Paolo Vercellini et al., 'Attractiveness of women with rectovaginal endometriosis: A case-control study', *Fertility and Sterility*, 99, 1 (2013), 10.1016/j.fertnstert.2012.08.039.
8. Nicola Slawson, '"Women have been woefully neglected": Does medical science have a gender problem?', *Guardian*, 18 December 2019, https://www.theguardian.com/

9 Lorena Rodrigo, 'Sperm genetic abnormalities and their contribution to embryo aneuploidy & miscarriage', *Best Practice & Research Clinical Endocrinology & Metabolism*, 34, 6, 2020, https://doi.org/10.1016/j.beem.2020.101477, Carlos Galaviz-Hernandez et al., 'Paternal determinants in preeclampsia', *Frontiers in Physiology*, 9, 1870 (2019), https://doi.org/10.3389/fphys.2018.01870.
10 https://www.nhs.uk/conditions/pataus-syndrome/.
11 Alastair Lee, *Pendle: Witch Country*, Vertebrate Publishing, 2019.
12 C. Galley, 'A never-ending succession of epidemics? Mortality in early-modern York', *Social History of Medicine*, 7, 1 (1994), 10.1093/shm/7.1.29.
13 Lucy Jones, *Matrescence: On the Metamorphosis of Pregnancy, Childbirth and Motherhood*, Penguin Books, 2024.
14 'Red fox mortality & disability', https://www.wildlifeonline.me.uk/animals/article/red-fox-mortality-disability.
15 Hans-Jörg Uther, 'The fox in world literature: Reflections on a "fictional animal"', *Asian Folklore Studies*, 65, 2 (2006).
16 Kerri ní Dochartaigh, *Thin Places*, Canongate Books, 2022.
17 Bodil Nildin-Wall and Jan Wall, 'The witch as hare or the witch's hare: Popular legends and beliefs in nordic tradition', *Folklore*, 104, 1/2 (1993), https://www.jstor.org/stable/1260796.

18 Robert Pitcairn, *Ancient Criminal Trials in Scotland, Vol. 3, Part 2*, Bannatyne Club, 1833.
19 'More bereaved parents offered baby-loss certificate', 9 October 2024, https://www.bbc.co.uk/news/articles/ce3zg2l512r0.
20 ONS, 'Abortion statistics for England and Wales: 2022' https://www.gov.uk/government/statistics/abortion-statistics-for-england-and-wales-2022, Public Health Scotland, 'Termination of pregnancy statistics', https://www.publichealthscotland.scot/publications/termination-of-pregnancy-statistics/termination-of-pregnancy-statistics-year-ending-december-2021/.
21 Suzanne Heaney et al., 'Pregnancy loss following miscarriage and termination of pregnancy for medical reasons during the COVID-19 pandemic: A thematic analysis of women's experiences of healthcare on the island of Ireland', *BMC Pregnancy and Childbirth*, 23, 529 (2023), https://bmcpregnancychildbirth.biomedcentral.com/articles/10.1186/s12884-023-05839-4#ref-CR9.